Step In!

Salesian Bible Meditations
Volume 1: The Old Testament

Meditations Written by Tom Vresics
Meditative Artwork by Amy Vresics

Kirsten
Parker

Dedicated to my loving wife Jan,
my amazing daughters Erin and Amy
and my supportive Salesian family throughout the world.

Live Jesus!

Why Salesian Lectio Divina?

It was 400 years ago that Saint Francis de Sales wrote the *Introduction to the Devout Life*. He wrote this book to help everyday people grow in holiness in ways thought to be restricted to only priests and religious in a monastery. The book's popularity grew because, in the words of Saint Francis de Sales, "....**the devotion which is true hinders nothing, but on the contrary it perfects everything; and that which runs counter to the rightful vocation of anyone is, you may be sure, a dubious devotion... everybody fulfils his special calling better when subject to the influence of devotion: -family duties are lighter, married love truer, service to our king more faithful, every kind of occupation more acceptable and better performed where that** (*devotion*) **is the guide."₁** Therefore, true devotion makes us better people, and who does not want that?

Recently, Pope Benedict XVI encouraged the practice of Lectio Divina in a pastoral letter marking the 40th anniversary of *Dei Verbum*. This prayer, once thought only to be appropriate for priests and religious, is now gaining popularity after Pope Benedict XVI recommended it for everyday modern Christians from all walks of life. Again, the words of Pope Benedict XVI say it best, "**If it** *(Lectio Divina)* **is effectively promoted, this practice will bring to the Church ... a new spiritual springtime. As a strong point of biblical ministry Lectio Divina should be increasingly encouraged."₂**

As part of the Year of Saint Paul, Bishop Michael Saltarelli of Wilmington echoed Pope Benedict XVI's call for Lectio Divina: "**This daily meditative prayer on the Sacred Scriptures engages thought, imagination, emotion and desire. This mobilization of our faculties deepens our convictions of faith, prompts the conversion of our hearts and strengthens our wills to follow Christ."₃**

This book seeks to combine the spiritual insights of Saint Francis de Sales within the framework of Lectio Divina. The idea is to help you, as a Christian teen, to see yourself and your experience mirrored in the stories of the Bible. As you place yourself in these stories, it is hoped that you will gain a deeper appreciation of God's goodness present in everyday life. I also hope that as you spend time alone with God in prayer, you will discover how profound God's love is for you as an individual amid the real circumstances of your life.

God Be Praised!

Table of Contents

The
Word
of God

Psalm 119:1-9,105

BEFORE WE BEGIN
Background Information

Have you ever received advice from a friend on how to succeed at an important task? Maybe it was how to solve Rubik's Cube or how to get the most from your cell phone. While at first you may have been happy to figure it out on your own, later you were happy for the tip.

This is what happened to young David who was not even considered important enough to be invited to a special family banquet with the prophet Samuel. Read 1 Samuel 16. Yet God saw a special greatness within his heart that even his own family missed. It was only because David took the Word of God into his heart that he was able to accomplish so much. No matter if it was the Word of God spoken through Moses or prophets like Samuel and Nathan, David was willing to be led by the Spirit of God. David's many spontaneous prayers in song, called the Psalms, reflect David's awareness of God's special presence throughout the ups and downs of David's life.

King David was not the only one to whom God offered guidance. Through our baptism all Christians have received the same Holy Spirit that inspired David to be his best and succeed. We, too, can live happier and healthier lives if we allow insights from pondering God's Word in our hearts to shape our future as David did.

Salesian Concept
Receiving the Word of God

Saint Francis de Sales was a man who was devoted to the Word of God. It is next to impossible to find any letter or chapter from his writings that does not contain a passage of Scripture or at least a reference to the Bible. Saint Francis continually reflected upon the Word of God in order to imitate Jesus, the Word made flesh.

As Salesians the easiest way to "**Live Jesus**"[4] is to follow the advice of Saint Francis, who wrote in the *Introduction to the Devout Life*, "**Be devoted to the Word of God whether you hear it in familiar conversations, with spiritual friends, or sermons. Always listen to it with attention and reverence; make good use of it; do not let it fall to earth but take it into your heart.**"[5]

In this meditation and those that follow, you will be asked to apply the lessons of Salesian prayer you have learned from De Sales, the Master of the Imagination, Heart and Virtue. See pages 105-110.

MEDITATION: A SALESIAN METHOD

1. Remote Preparation

    a. Throw off all your concerns from the school day. *(Relax)*
    b. Read Psalm 119: 1-9, 105 below.

Happy those whose way is blameless, who walk by the teaching of the LORD. Happy those who observe God's decrees, who seek the LORD with all their heart.

They do no wrong; they walk in God's ways. You have given them the command to keep your precepts with care.

May my ways be firm in the observance of your laws! Then I will not be ashamed to ponder all your commands. I will praise you with a sincere heart as I study your just edicts. I will keep your laws; do not leave me all alone.

How can the young walk without fault? Only by keeping your word ... your word is a lamp for my feet and a light for my path.

2. Immediate Preparation

    a. Ask for a deeper awareness of God's presence.
    b. Ask for God's inspiration to pray sincerely.

3. Considerations *(Write down your insights about God's goodness to us.)*

Imagine that you are young David reflecting on this Psalm after writing it. You think about your ancestors in faith like Abraham. He faced the hardship in leaving his father 's family in Mesopotamia to make a Covenant with an unseen God. As a result he and his wife Sarah received many descendants, land and prosperity. How willing are you to be led by God even though you cannot physically see God?

You later think about Joseph who was sold into slavery by his brothers. As you think of how he made the best of a bad situation to become Governor of Egypt, how are you inspired to blamelessly follow the teachings of the Lord in difficult times?

As you gaze out over your family's sheep, you notice some straying away from the herd. After rounding them up, you recall how the Israelites strayed from the Ten Commandments while in the desert. What motivates you to be different from them in your life?

As you start leading your sheep home, you have to cross a small stream. It reminds you of Joshua leading the Israelites into the Promised Land of Canaan. You recall the words of Joshua telling the people to keep the laws of the covenant faithfully. What stories from Joshua demonstrate God's faithfulness to the covenant? What stories from the times of the Judges, like Samson, serve as a warning not to be ashamed to ponder God's commands and praise him with a sincere heart?

As you think of your future, what thoughts come to mind as you reflect on your own words, "How can the young walk without fault? Only by keeping your word...Your word is a lamp for my feet and a light for my path."

4. Affections *(Write a three sentence spontaneous, heartfelt prayer.)*

What are you feeling as you see David thinking about his life with God before he accomplished any of his great deeds? What are your feelings about the value of the Word of God and its role in shaping your life? What can you say to God to help you plan for your own future?

5. Resolution *(Write a resolution describing what you will do and when.)*

What do you feel you should do in order to live this day well in light of your meditation? Write one concrete resolution that can serve as your response to the Word of God in your life.

6. TOP-Off *(Thanksgiving / Offering / Petition)*

a. Give thanksgiving to God for this experience of calm.

b. Offer to God your resolution of ....

c. Ask God to give you the grace to accomplish this.

7. Word Art *(Draw an image with words to help you recall your prayer time.)*

Pick any word, phrase or image from this meditation that can help you remember your time with God today. This word and/or image should also help you gratefully fulfill your resolution to follow the Word of God in your heart and to allow it to shape your life.

1. Remote Preparation Check Box ☐

2. Immediate Preparation Check Box ☐

3. **Considerations** *(Write down your insights about God and this story.)*

_____

_____

_____

_____

_____

_____

_____

_____

_____

_____

_____

_____

_____

4. Affections *(Write a three sentence spontaneous, heartfelt prayer.)*

_____

_____

_____

_____

_____

_____

5. Resolution *(Write a resolution that describes what you will do and when.)*

_____

_____

_____

6. TOP-Off *(Thanksgiving / Offering / Petition)* **Check Box** ☐

7. Word Art *(Draw an image with words to help you recall your prayer time.)*

The Priestly Creation Story

Genesis 1:26-28,31

BEFORE WE BEGIN

Background Information

Have you ever felt that the people placed in charge of you, like your principal, a least favorite teacher, and/or a demanding coach, thought that you were good for nothing? How did they make you feel? Did you ever lose your confidence because of them?

When the Jews returned from being slaves in Babylon over 500 years before the birth of Christ, many Jews recalled how the Babylonians tormented them. Read Psalm 137:1-9. Most Babylonians believed that only the powerful deserved to be treated with respect. While the Jews could see how powerful the warlike Babylonians were, they also knew that the Babylonians were not happy people.

After the Exile, the Jews renewed their religious identity by putting together the Torah. The Torah explains the covenant that made the Jews God's Chosen People. The Genesis creation stories not only contradicted the Babylonian world view, but also showed how the right relationship with God and others is better than power.

See if you can pick out the ways the Genesis Creation stories sought to reverse the poor self-image of the former slaves. In light of the above, realize that these creation stories are more about what it means to be a human than they are about how long it took God to create the universe.

Salesian Concept
Salesian Optimism

One of the most fundamental teachings of Saint Francis de Sales is that as humans we are fundamentally good because we are all created in the image and likeness of God.

Saint Francis de Sales had several reasons for this belief. First, he taught that Jesus would have become human even if our first parents had never sinned. Saint Francis arrived at this conclusion based upon his reflection on the nature of love which seeks union with its beloved.

Second, Saint Francis taught that since Jesus was fully human and never sinned, there is no part of our humanity that is essentially sinful. This means that any human activity, like eating, can lead us closer to God if we do God's will as Jesus did. This is why as a Salesian you are called to be optimistic about life, seek to **"Live Jesus"** in every present moment and strive to **"be who you are and be that well in order to give glory to the Master craftsman whose handiwork you are."**[6]

11

MEDITATION: A SALESIAN METHOD

1. Remote Preparation

a. Throw off all your concerns from the school day. *(Relax)*
b. Read Genesis 1:26-28, 31 below.

Then God said: "Let us make man in our image, after our likeness. Let them have dominion over the fish of the sea, the birds of the air, and the cattle, and over all the wild animals and all the creatures that crawl on the ground."

God created man in his image; in the divine image he created him; male and female he created them. God blessed them, saying: "Be fertile and multiply; fill the earth and subdue it. Have dominion over the fish of the sea, the birds of the air, and all the living things that move on the earth." ....And so it happened. God looked at everything he had made, and he found it very good. Evening came, and morning followed the sixth day.

2. Immediate Preparation

a. Ask for a deeper awareness of God's presence.
b. Ask for God's inspiration to pray sincerely.

3. Considerations *(Write down your insights about God's goodness to us.)*

Imagine that you are there on the sixth day of creation. Picture all the goodness of the earth: the vastness of the oceans, the beauty of rainbows, the majesty of great snowcapped mountains, plus the awesome wonders of waterfalls, canyons and forests.

Think of all the diversity of sizes, colors and abilities found in the animal kingdom. Think of the various species of birds and fish, plus the different varieties of animals. Why are all these wonders of creation, the birds, the fish and the animals not enough for God?

Listen to God the Father say to his Son, the Word who became flesh and the Holy Spirit, the Breath of God, "Let us make man in our image, after our likeness." What is their shared reaction at the creation of the first man and woman? What are their hopes for our first parents? What are their hopes for every new human life?

Now, God the Father blesses the first man and woman and tells them to be fruitful and multiply. What goodness does God see in the sexual powers he gave to our first parents and to us?

What is the facial expression on the first man and first woman when the Father gives them dominion over the fish, birds and the animals on the earth, but not over one another?

God the Father declares the goodness of our humanity. What expressions do the man and woman have? What kind of facial expression and heartfelt emotions do you have?

4. Affections *(Write a three sentence spontaneous, heartfelt prayer.)*

What are you feeling as you see our first parents? What can you say in gratitude to God for the gift of human life? What are your feelings about being made in the image and likeness of God, despite sometimes failing to reflect that image and likeness in your actions?

5. Resolution *(Write a resolution describing what you will do and when.)*

What do you feel you should do in order to live this day well in light of your meditation? Write one concrete resolution that can serve as your response to live according to the image and likeness of God.

6. TOP-Off *(Thanksgiving / Offering / Petition)*

a. Give thanksgiving to God for this experience of calm.

b. Offer to God your resolution of ....

c. Ask God to give you the grace to accomplish this.

7. Word Art *(Draw an image with words to help you recall your prayer time.)*

Pick any word, phrase or image from this meditation that can help you remember your time with the Trinity today. This word and/or image should also help you gratefully fulfill your resolution to live according to the image and likeness of God.

1. Remote Preparation Check Box ☐

2. Immediate Preparation Check Box ☐

3. **Considerations** *(Write down your insights about God and this story.)*

_____

_____

_____

_____

_____

_____

_____

_____

_____

_____

_____

_____

4. Affections *(Write a three sentence spontaneous, heartfelt prayer.)*

_____

_____

_____

_____

_____

_____

5. Resolution *(Write a resolution that describes what you will do and when.)*

_____

_____

_____

6. TOP-Off *(Thanksgiving / Offering / Petition)* **Check Box** ☐

7. Word Art *(Draw an image with words to help you recall your prayer time.)*

The
Call of
Abram

Genesis 12:1-3a, 4-7

BEFORE WE BEGIN

Background Information

Recall a time when parents or teachers promised you something you really wanted. All you had to do was take a risk and go the distance. What initial doubts did you have? At any time, did you feel that you had made a mistake? Were your efforts rewarded properly?

The risk that Abram and Sarai took was to believe in an unseen God. During their time people worshipped various parts of nature, like the sun or the moon. They could see, however, that everything in nature is subject to something else. The sun may have the power to melt snow from a storm, but winter storm clouds have the power to block out the sun for days. Abram and Sarai realized, therefore, that the creator of the universe had to be greater than any visible part of it. Abraham became our Father in Faith because together with his wife Sarai, he was willing to act on his belief and faithfully journey with an unseen God.

Of course, we know that their efforts were rewarded by God. He and his wife were given new names, Abraham and Sarah. They were blessed with prosperity, the Promised Land of Canaan, and numerous descendants, beginning with their son Isaac. However, Abraham's and Sarah's most important descendant was Jesus, through whom God blessed every nation on earth.

We will all be credited with faith and righteousness by God if we follow Abraham and Sarah's example to walk with God despite our doubts.

Salesian Concept
True Devotion

In the *Introduction to the Devout Life* Saint Francis de Sales states that "true and living devotion . . . is simply a true love of God."[7] In short, true devotion is spiritual liveliness by which we do God's Will promptly, diligently, and often. De Sales uses a bird analogy to teach about different levels of devotion. He writes "**Consider birds. Ostriches never fly; chickens fly, but rarely, heavily and low; eagles, doves and swallows fly often, swiftly and high.**"[8] To be devout we should seek God as eagles seek the heights.

If we are truly devout, we will continue to do God's Will in the various present moments in our lives. This means obeying our parents promptly, cleaning our rooms or doing our homework diligently, and going to Mass and helping the less fortunate as often as possible.

MEDITATION: A SALESIAN METHOD

1. Remote Preparation

a. Throw off all your concerns from the school day. *(Relax)*
b. Read Genesis 15:1-3a, 4-7 below.

Some time after these events, this word of the LORD came to Abram in a vision: "Fear not, Abram! I am your shield; I will make your reward very great." But Abram said, "O Lord GOD, what good will your gifts be, if I keep on being childless? See, you have given me no offspring, and so one of my servants will be my heir."

Then the word of the LORD came to him: "No, that one shall not be your heir; your own issue shall be your heir." He took him outside and said: "Look up at the sky and count the stars, if you can. Just so," he added, "shall your descendants be."

Abram put his faith in the LORD, who credited it to him as an act of righteousness. He then said to him, "I am the LORD who brought you from Ur of the Chaldeans to give you this land as a possession."

2. Immediate Preparation

a. Ask for a deeper awareness of God's presence.
b. Ask for God's inspiration to pray sincerely.

3. Considerations *(Write down your insights about how God eased Abram's doubt and helped him grow in faith.)*

Imagine that you are with Abram as he speaks with God. Listen to the silence that allowed Abram to sense the presence of God in the midst of the barely populated land of Canaan.

Now picture all the stars in the sky, more visible than the starriest night you have ever seen due to the lack of light pollution in the ancient world. How does this help you see that as awesome as this sight is, the greatness of God far surpasses it?

Imagine Abram's reaction as God tells him that his servant Eliezer will not inherit everything, but that God will grant Abram a child of his own with his wife Sarai. How does this make him feel?

As Abram continues to ponder God's promises while gazing at the countless stars overhead, he begins to realize that his journey with God is far from over. He and Sarai will continually face new challenges that can only be overcome by seeking and loving God promptly, diligently, and often. What is scary about the realization that their journey with God is not once and done? What is consoling about the promise of God's love throughout their long journey? What is exciting about the promise of those many descendants and God's covenant with Abram and Sarai for their faith and trust in God?

4. Affections *(Write a three sentence spontaneous, heartfelt prayer.)*

What are you feeling as you see Abram standing under the countless stars of the ancient sky? What can you say to God as a promise to seek his presence in your life promptly, diligently, and often, no matter what may happen in your life?

5. Resolution *(Write a resolution that describes what you will do and when.)*

What do you feel you should do in order to live this day well in light of your meditation? Write one concrete resolution that can serve as your response to always seek God in your life.

6. TOP-Off *(Thanksgiving / Offering / Petition)*

a. Give thanksgiving to God for this experience of calm.
b. Offer to God your resolution of ....
c. Ask God to give you the grace to accomplish this.

7. Word Art *(Draw an image with words to help you recall your prayer.)*

Pick any word, phrase or image from this meditation that can help you remember your time with God today. This word and/or image should also help you diligently fulfill your resolution to continually seek God's presence and will, despite any doubts you may have.

1. Remote Preparation Check Box ☐

2. Immediate Preparation Check Box ☐

3. **Considerations** *(Write down your insights about God and this story.)*

_____

_____

_____

_____

_____

_____

_____

_____

_____

_____

_____

_____

4. Affections *(Write a three sentence spontaneous, heartfelt prayer.)*

_____

_____

_____

_____

_____

_____

5. Resolution *(Write a resolution that describes what you will do and when.)*

_____

_____

_____

6. TOP-Off *(Thanksgiving / Offering / Petition)* **Check Box** ☐

7. Word Art *(Draw an image with words to help you recall your prayer time.)*

The Birth of Isaac

Genesis 21:1-8

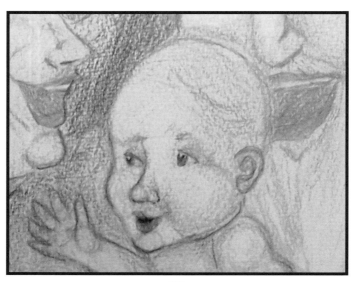

BEFORE WE BEGIN
Background Information
Have you ever taken a short cut in doing a chore your parents left to you rather than following their exact directions? Have you ever failed a test because you read the Spark Notes version rather than reading the whole book? Maybe you skipped off-season conditioning and then failed to make a team in which you had the talent to excel.

Think of the happiness you would have missed if your parents used the chore and or novel exam as the test of your readiness to do something great, like get a fun job with friends that paid really well. Or how would you feel if the team went on to win a championship without you? In either case, the purpose of these challenges was to help lead you to greater happiness and fulfillment.

This is what happened to Abraham and Sarah. God promised them many descendants, but they used an easier way without God. Fortunately for them, God overlooked their attempt to use the common and legal practice of the day to use a surrogate mother to give them a son. Instead God gave them joy beyond all telling when God allowed them to have a son through natural means. Their joy was so great that they named their son Isaac, which means *"He will laugh"* or *"God will smile"* in Hebrew. God's ways are perfect and just; our ways often fall short.

Salesian Concept
The Signified Will of God
Saint Francis de Sales taught that one way God expresses his will for us is through the Signified Will of God as expressed in the Scriptures such as the 10 Commandments and the Beatitudes of Jesus. The Signified Will of God is also expressed in Church teachings like attending Mass on Sundays and Holy Days of Obligation.

The second aspect of the Signified Will of God is fulfilling our duties. De Sales wrote in a memo cited in *Letters of Spiritual Direction*, **"Anyone who does not do this** (*carry out the duties of one's vocation*) **with care can possess nothing but a fraudulent devotion."**[9] As a student this means faithfully keeping your school's dress code and honestly completing all homework, tests and service work.

The third aspect of the Signified Will of God includes those things over which you have no control, like what your mother makes for dinner. No matter what she makes the Fourth Commandment, "Honor your father and mother" still applies.

23

MEDITATION: A SALESIAN METHOD

1. Remote Preparation

a. Throw off all your concerns from the school day. *(Relax)*
b. Read Genesis 21:1-8.

The LORD took note of Sarah as he had said he would; he did for her as he had promised. Sarah became pregnant and bore Abraham a son in his old age, at the set time that God had stated. Abraham gave the name Isaac to this son of his whom Sarah bore him. When his son Isaac was eight days old, Abraham circumcised him, as God had commanded. Abraham was a hundred years old when his son Isaac was born to him. Sarah then said, "God has given me cause to laugh, and all who hear of it will laugh with me. Who would have told Abraham," she added, "that Sarah would nurse children! Yet I have borne him a son in his old age." Isaac grew, and on the day of the child's weaning, Abraham held a great feast.

2. Immediate Preparation

a. Ask for a deeper awareness of God's presence.
b. Ask for God's inspiration to pray sincerely.

3. Considerations *(Write down your insights about God's goodness.)*

Imagine that you are Abraham and Sarah on the day of Isaac's birth. How is Sarah's joy increased by the fact that God's blessings upon Abraham have now been given to her as well? How is Abraham's joy completed by the birth of a son to fully pass on the blessings of his and Sarah's covenant with God to all their descendants?

Think of all the thoughts Abraham and Sarah have as they recall the circumstances that led them to leave Haran in the first place. Imagine the ridicule they faced from neighbors and former friends when they talked to them about following a God no one could see. Imagine the difficulties they faced as they moved to the unfamiliar land of Canaan, the fear of the unknown, the distance, etc. What do you think they would recall as the most difficult parts of their journey of faith?

Now, listen to Abraham and Sarah's son Isaac make the sounds that every newborn infant makes. What facial expressions do Abraham and Sarah share in this tender heartfelt moment?

What are the reactions of people at the feast to the fact that Sarah is 100 years old and having her first child? What are they saying to her? What does Sarah say in response to their amazement?

Isaac cries as he is circumcised. How do Abraham and Sarah comfort him? How do their facial expressions reflect their newfound knowledge that wonderful and unexpected blessings follow those who faithfully trust in God during times of difficulty and suffering?

4. Affections *(Write a three sentence spontaneous, heartfelt prayer.)*

What are you feeling as you see Abraham and Sarah with Isaac? What can you say to God for the times you failed to place your total trust in Him or sought to do things your own way rather than following God's way?

5. Resolution *(Write a resolution that describes what you will do and when.)*

What do you feel you should do in order to live this day well in light of your meditation? Write one concrete resolution that can serve as your response to accept hardships while seeking God's blessings.

6. TOP-Off *(Thanksgiving / Offering / Petition)*

a. Give thanksgiving to God for this experience of calm.

b. Offer to God your resolution of ....

c. Ask God to give you the grace to accomplish this.

7. Word Art *(Draw an image with words to help you recall your prayer.)*

Pick any word, phrase or image from this meditation that can help you remember your time with God today. This word and/or image should also help you gratefully fulfill your resolution to live with more faith and trust in God in the midst of difficulties.

1. Remote Preparation Check Box ☐

2. Immediate Preparation Check Box ☐

3. Considerations *(Write down your insights about God and this story.)*

_____

_____

_____

_____

_____

_____

_____

_____

_____

_____

4. Affections *(Write a three sentence spontaneous, heartfelt prayer.)*

_____

_____

_____

_____

_____

_____

5. Resolution *(Write a resolution that describes what you will do and when.)*

_____

_____

_____

6. TOP-Off *(Thanksgiving / Offering / Petition)* **Check Box** ☐

7. Word Art *(Draw an image with words to help you recall your prayer.)*

Joseph
In
Egypt

Genesis 45:4-10

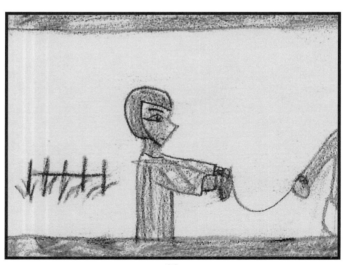

BEFORE WE BEGIN
Background Information

Do you benefit from favoritism or do you mainly fall victim to it? Favoritism causes hurt in families, among friends, at school and in the work place, but it is not the deciding factor in how successful we will be. No matter on what side of the favored treatment you fall, receiving special favors does not make you better than anyone else, and being overlooked does not mean that you should stop trying to be your best.

Abraham's family suffered greatly from the effects of favoritism. Isaac's favoritism towards the more athletic Esau led his wife Rebecca to favor their younger son, Jacob. With Rebecca's help, Jacob was able to steal Esau's birthright and blessing. Read Genesis 25-33 for details.

In turn, Jacob favored his youngest son Joseph over his other eleven sons. When Joseph received a special long tunic or coat from his father Jacob, it signified that Joseph was free from the burden of manual labor. Not surprisingly, this caused jealousy and resentment among Joseph's older brothers who worked in the fields while he just supervised.

Oddly enough, Jacob's favoritism towards Joseph did not guarantee success. After being sold into slavery in Egypt, Joseph was continually placed in new situations where he had to begin anew and prove himself. Only by accepting God's help was Joseph able to succeed.

Salesian Concept
The Present Moment from the Spiritual Directory

Saint Francis desired to grow in holiness by doing God's Will in every present moment of his day. The *Spiritual Directory* is the guide for daily living he created to find God in each moment and to be his best in all his daily activities. For example, when waking up rather than saying, "Oh darn! It's Monday!" he would say, "**Sleep is the image of death and rising** *(or waking up)* **the image of the resurrection.**"[10]

According to Francis there is no part of our day when we cannot find God or benefit from his grace. In the final part of *Introduction to the Devout Life* on renewing one's desire to live a devout life, Saint Francis wrote, "**When the road of holiness seems difficult to you, repeat after Saint Francis of Assisi: 'All the troubles and all the sufferings of this earth are nothing compared to the blessings to come.'**[11] In both good or bad times, this teaching can lead us to success.

MEDITATION: A SALESIAN METHOD

1. Remote Preparation

a. Throw off all your concerns from the school day. *(Relax)*
b. Read Genesis 45:4-10.

"I am your brother Joseph, whom you once sold into Egypt. But now do not be distressed, and do not reproach yourselves for having sold me here. It was really for the sake of saving lives that God sent me here ahead of you."

"For two years now the famine has been in the land, and for five more years tillage will yield no harvest. God, therefore, sent me on ahead of you to ensure for you a remnant on earth and to save your lives in an extraordinary deliverance. So it was not really you but God who had me come here; and he has made of me a father to Pharaoh, lord of all his household, and ruler over the whole land of Egypt."

"Hurry back, then, to my father and tell him: 'Thus says your son Joseph: God has made me lord of all Egypt; come to me without delay. You will settle in the region of Goshen, where you will be near me, you and your children and grandchildren, your flocks and herds, and everything that you own.'"

2. Immediate Preparation

a. Ask for a deeper awareness of God's presence.
b. Ask for God's inspiration to pray sincerely.

3. Considerations *(Write down your insights about God's goodness.)*

Imagine that you are Joseph recalling all the events that led to this moment. Think about all the ups and downs you encountered as you went from being your father's favorite to being a slave, from being a slave to being placed in charge of Potipher's house, from earning that level of trust to being thrown in jail, from being in prison to serving as Governor of Egypt. How has your trust in God's presence helped you?

You recall your dreams and the resentment they caused, first the dream of your brothers' sheaves of wheat bowing to yours and then their stars bowing to your star. How have these dreams been fulfilled by God?

You begin to think of your most difficult times, like when you first arrived in Egypt as a slave or when you were falsely accused of raping Potipher's wife and thrown in jail. As you remember just how scared you were, you also recall that each time you just took a deep breath and resolved to make the best of a bad situation. How did focusing upon doing your best rather than brooding over the wrongs that led to your difficulties help you succeed in each new present moment?

Now you hug your brothers and begin to feel the healing that true reconciliation brings. How have your experiences prepared you to be a better brother? How much more appreciative are you for the blessings of family life? How has your trust in God's providence and care grown?

4. Affections *(Write a three sentence spontaneous, heartfelt prayer.)*

What are you feeling as you see Joseph happy to be reunited with his brothers? What can you say to God for the times you failed to seek his presence and help during your biggest difficulties? What can you say to show proper gratitude to God for all he has given you to succeed in life like your family?

5. Resolution *(Write a resolution that describes what you will do and when.)*

What do you feel you should do in order to live this day well in light of your meditation? Write one concrete resolution that can serve as your response to God's constant presence in both good and bad times.

6. TOP-Off *(Thanksgiving / Offering / Petition)*

a. Give thanksgiving to God for this experience of calm.

b. Offer to God your resolution of ....

c. Ask God to give you the grace to accomplish this.

7. Word Art *(Draw an image with words to help you recall your prayer.)*

Pick any word, phrase or image from this meditation that can help you remember your time with God today. This word and/or image should also help you gratefully fulfill your resolution to find God and ask his help to be your best in all the present moments of your life.

"It was really for the sake of saving lives that God sent me here ahead of you." Genesis 45:5

1. Remote Preparation Check Box ☐

2. Immediate Preparation Check Box ☐

3. Considerations *(Write down your insights about God and this story.)*

_____

_____

_____

_____

_____

_____

_____

_____

_____

_____

_____

_____

4. Affections *(Write a three sentence spontaneous, heartfelt prayer.)*

_____

_____

_____

_____

_____

_____

5. Resolution *(Write a resolution that describes what you will do and when.)*

_____

_____

_____

6. TOP-Off *(Thanksgiving / Offering / Petition)* **Check Box** ☐

7. Word Art *(Draw an image with words to help you recall your prayer.)*

The Call of Moses

Exodus 3:1-12

BEFORE WE BEGIN

Background Information

Have you ever been spared from something terrible that caused your friends much hardship? Perhaps you avoided getting a teacher who gave way too much homework and impossible tests. Morally, there is not much you are required to do, but thank God. But what if you knew innocent people were experiencing inhumane suffering due to the selfishness, greed or thoughtlessness of humanity?

This is what Moses experienced. He was spared from slavery by his mother's quick thinking and raised by Pharaoh. However, when he saw the cruelty the Hebrews received from their Egyptian taskmasters, his conscience led Moses to take a stand on their behalf.

Moses failed miserably in his first attempt because he acted alone. He was quickly discovered by Pharaoh and exiled to the Midian desert. However, with God's help and people like Aaron, Moses would later return to free the Hebrew slaves to worship the LORD or "I AM WHO AM" on the very mountain from which God called him in today's story.

Often we are challenged to stand up for the oppressed. It may be the poor, war orphans, or the unborn. Following God's call often means risking being mistreated ourselves. To succeed, we all need to listen for God's voice in our consciences. Luckily, we will never have to fight alone due to all the social justice organizations in the Church that expose injustice and mobilize Christians to act for a more just world.

Salesian Concept

Justice

When Saint Francis de Sales speaks of the responsibility of justice in the *Introduction to the Devout Life* he cautions us against having a double standard for judging all situations towards our advantage. Rather Saint Francis de Sales tells Philothea, **"Be just in all your actions ... Always put yourself in your neighbor's place, and put your neighbor's in yours, and then you will judge fairly."**[12] He continues saying, **"Examine your heart often ... to be assured that it is behaving towards your neighbor as you would like his to behave towards you."**[13] As Salesians whenever we may grow tired of seeking to **"Live Jesus,"** we might also recall the words of Jesus in the Parable of the Sheep and Goats in Matthew 24:45, "What you did for one of these least brothers (*and sisters*) of mine, you did for me."

MEDITATION: A SALESIAN METHOD

1. Remote Preparation

a. Throw off all your concerns from the school day. *(Relax)*
b. Read Exodus 3:1-12. *(Below is only a brief excerpt.)*

Moses was leading the flock across the desert; he came to Horeb, the mountain of God. There an angel of the LORD appeared to him in fire flaming out of a bush. Moses was surprised that the bush, though on fire, was not consumed.

So Moses decided, "I must go over to look at this remarkable sight." God called out to him from the bush, "Moses! Moses!" He answered, "Here I am."

The LORD said, "I have witnessed the affliction of my people in Egypt and have heard their cry of complaint against their slave drivers."

"Come, now! I will send you to Pharaoh to lead my people, the Israelites, out of Egypt." But Moses said to God, "Who am I that I should go to Pharaoh and lead the Israelites out of Egypt?"

God answered, "I will be with you; and this shall be your proof that it is I who have sent you: when you bring my people out of Egypt, you will worship Me on this very mountain."

2. Immediate Preparation

a. Ask for a deeper awareness of God's presence.
b. Ask for God's inspiration to pray sincerely.

3. Considerations *(Write down your insights about how God calls us to justice.)*

Imagine that you are Moses safe from Pharaoh's reach as long as you stay in Midian with your new father-in-law's flocks. Amidst the bleating of the sheep and your concern for your new family, you can hardly recall the suffering of the Hebrew slaves in Egypt. What are you most grateful for in your newfound situation?

Suddenly, you see a large bush engulfed in fire on a high mountain peak. Surprisingly after a long period of time, it is still burning as fiercely as it was from the time you first noticed it. You climb up the peak to investigate it. The height from the peak of the mountain reminds you of the pyramids of Egypt and the cruelty of the Egyptians towards the Hebrew slaves. What images and sounds fill your mind as you look across the desert of Midian towards Egypt? What suppressed feelings come to the surface of your conscience?

As you take in these emotions, you hear the voice from the burning bush telling you to lead the Hebrews out of slavery in Egypt. What doubts do you have? How does God's call meet with your deepest desire to make good come from the sacrifice your mother made to save your life by placing you in a basket on the Nile?

As you hear that the sign of the reality of this call is that the Hebrew slaves will worship God on the very mountain upon which you are standing, what sacrifices and risks come to mind? What sense of strength and hope fills your mind and heart as you stand before God in this holy place?

4. Affections *(Write a three sentence spontaneous, heartfelt prayer.)*

What are you feeling as you see the burning bush and look across Sinai's height across the desert to the land of Egypt? What can you say to God for the strength to leave your comfort zone in order to respond to the suffering you see in the world or on the evening news?

5. Resolution *(Write a resolution that describes what you will do and when.)*

What do you feel you should do in order to live this day well in light of your meditation? Write one concrete resolution that can serve as your response to heed God's call to take risks to help the oppressed.

6. TOP-Off *(Thanksgiving / Offering / Petition)*

a. Give thanksgiving to God for this experience of calm.

b. Offer to God your resolution of ....

c. Ask God to give you the grace to accomplish this.

7. Word Art *(Draw an image with words to help you recall this prayer time.)*

Pick any word, phrase or image from this meditation that can help you remember your time with God today. This word and/or image should also help you gratefully fulfill your resolution to take a risk to respond to God's call to help those suffering from serious injustices.

"I have witnessed the affliction of my people in Egypt and have heard the cry of their complaint against their slave drivers."

1. Remote Preparation Check Box ☐

2. Immediate Preparation Check Box ☐

3. **Considerations** *(Write down your insights about God and this story.)*

_____

_____

_____

_____

_____

_____

_____

_____

_____

_____

_____

4. Affections *(Write a three sentence spontaneous, heartfelt prayer.)*

_____

_____

_____

_____

_____

_____

5. Resolution *(Write a resolution that describes what you will do and when.)*

_____

_____

_____

6. TOP-Off *(Thanksgiving / Offering / Petition)* **Check Box** ☐

7. Word Art *(Draw an image with words to help you recall your prayer time.)*

Israel Enters the Promised Land

Joshua 24:1-2a, 13-15

BEFORE WE BEGIN

Background Information

Have you ever had to make a stand for your faith in God? Maybe your friends were discussing whether or not they go to Mass or who was actually going to sign up to do service work organized by your church. You probably felt put on the spot as everyone turned to hear you. Maybe you felt embarrassed to say that these things, while not as fun or exciting as hanging out, were still very important to you.

This is what the Israelites faced as they entered the Promised Land of Canaan. Joshua was not as much of a commanding figure as Moses and since Moses was no longer there to keep everyone in line, people felt more freedom to go their own way.

Joshua stood up to remind the Israelites that their newfound freedom should not be used to forget about the many great deeds God had and still continued to do for them. History shows that Joshua's speech not only inspired the Israelites to greater faithfulness, but also led poorer Canaanites to follow Israel's God as well. These Canaanites were attracted to the Israelite sense of justice that all people were equally responsible to follow God's Law. Canaanite leaders were never held accountable for their misdeeds.

As you grow older, you will be given more freedom to choose whether or not you will honor and serve God. Your choice today is no less important than the one Joshua and Israel made so long ago.

Salesian Concept
Love of Complacency

Saint Francis de Sales chose the humble and gentle heart of Jesus in Matthew 11 for his primary image of Jesus. It should be no surprise then that Salesian Spirituality sees our hearts as the center of our spiritual journey towards God.

In the *Treatise on the Love of God* Book V, Chapter 9, Saint Francis writes, "**Love of complacency draws the divine sweetness into our heart, which so ardently fills itself there with that it is overcharged.**"[14] In other words, when we acknowledge all the good God has done for us, love of complacency fills our hearts and prompts us to praise God. The more we meditate upon God's goodness to us, the more likely we are to use our freedom to honor and serve God.

MEDITATION: A SALESIAN METHOD

1. Remote Preparation

    a. Throw off all your concerns from the school day. *(Relax)*
    b. Read Joshua 24:1-2a, 13-15.

Joshua gathered together all the tribes of Israel at Shechem. When they stood in ranks before God, Joshua addressed all the people: ..."Thus says the LORD, the God of Israel: I gave you a land which you had not tilled and cities which you had not built to dwell in; you have eaten of vineyards and olive groves which you did not plant. Now, therefore, fear the LORD and serve him completely and sincerely. Cast out the gods your fathers served beyond the River and in Egypt, and serve the LORD. If it does not please you to serve the LORD, decide today whom you will serve, the gods your fathers served beyond the river or the gods of the Amorites in whose country you are dwelling. As for me and my household, we will serve the LORD."

2. Immediate Preparation

    a. Ask for a deeper awareness of God's presence.
    b. Ask for God's inspiration to pray sincerely.

3. Considerations *(Write down your insights about the importance of God.)*

    Imagine that you are with Joshua and the Chosen People as they entered the Promised Land of Canaan. Think of the numerous deeds of God. What images come to mind as you recall the following: the plagues through which God defeated the gods of Egypt, your family eating the Passover Meal of roasted lamb with unleavened bread and bitter herbs, crossing of the Red Sea as the Egyptian army closed in on you, the joyful song Miriam sang after you all safely escaped the Egyptian army, your victory over the Amalakites when the Israelites got the better of the fight whenever Moses held his arms up in prayer, God miraculously feeding you with manna and quail in the desert, Moses striking a rock at the command of God and water gushing forth to silence your complaints or receiving the Ten Commandments from Moses on Mount Sinai?

Now, listen to Joshua as he states that the Lord is even doing more for you by giving you this land filled with vineyards and cities ready to sustain a happy life. Who has done more for you or given you more reasons to be thankful than God?

How do others react as they realize that the Lord has remained faithful and good even after they worshipped the golden calf and constantly doubted Moses' instructions from God? What emotions do you have as you recall your unfaithfulness to God?

Joshua states that he and his family shall serve the Lord. What is your decision on whom you will serve through your life's actions? How can you start serving God right now?

4. Affections *(Write a three sentence spontaneous, heartfelt prayer.)*

What are you feeling as you pledge your service to God? What can you say to God as a pledge to rid your heart of selfishness? How can you use your freedom to serve God in both good times and bad times?

5. Resolution *(Write a resolution that describes what you will do and when.)*

What do you feel you should do in order to live this day well in light of your meditation? Write one concrete resolution that can serve as your response to freely serve God for his goodness to you.

6. TOP-Off *(Thanksgiving / Offering / Petition)*

a. Give thanksgiving to God for this experience of calm.
b. Offer to God your resolution of ....
c. Ask God to give you the grace to accomplish this.

7. Word Art *(Draw an image with words to help your recall your prayer time.)*

Pick any word, phrase or image from this meditation that can help you remember your time with God today. This word and/or image should also help you gratefully fulfill your resolution to serve God and remove anything that keeps you from following God's ways.

1. Remote Preparation Check Box ☐

2. Immediate Preparation Check Box ☐

3. **Considerations** *(Write down your insights about God and this story.)*

_____

_____

_____

_____

_____

_____

_____

_____

_____

_____

_____

_____

_____

4. Affections *(Write a three sentence spontaneous, heartfelt prayer.)*

_____

_____

_____

_____

_____

_____

5. Resolution *(Write a resolution that describes what you will do and when.)*

_____

_____

_____

6. TOP-Off *(Thanksgiving / Offering / Petition)* **Check Box** ☐

7. Word Art *(Draw an image with words to help you recall your prayer time.)*

David
Defeats
Goliath

1 Samuel 17:40-51

BEFORE WE BEGIN
Background Information

What is the scariest thing that you have ever had to face alone? Maybe it was walking home alone on a dark night, or speaking in public or confronting a teacher about something that wasn't right. No matter what it was, if you are reading this now, you survived it.

Think of how the situation eventually got to the point where you had to overcome your fears and believe in yourself or your goals in order to succeed. This is what David had to do to defeat Goliath.

God had promised his Chosen People prosperity in the land of Israel. Now Goliath and the Philistines stood in the way of that goal by oppressing the Israelites. Through the Sinai Covenant with Moses, God had set up the means for the Israelites to stand up to any danger by remaining faithful to God and to one another. Unfortunately, King Saul now only thought about being king and feared anything or anyone, like Goliath, that could take that kingdom away.

Fortunately for Israel, young David was filled with the spirit of the Lord from his recent anointing by Samuel in Bethlehem (1 Sm. 16). While we will always have to face frightening things in life, knowing God is always near can help us bravely face our most difficult times.

Salesian Concept
Sayings on Courage by Saint Francis de Sales

How many times do we lose courage when things go wrong? Saint Francis de Sales, who faced death on more than one occasion, is often quoted as saying, "Let the waves roar. Let the wind blow. Let the whole world turn upside down. Let everything be in uproar. Nothing can hurt you, God is near."[15]

Often we can think that our lives should be free of any trouble. In *The Golden Counsels* Saint Francis is quoted, "Do not fear evil... if evil should come, God will strengthen you. If God commands you to walk upon the waves of adversity do not doubt; do not be afraid. God is with you; have courage and you will be delivered."[16]

Finally, to avoid taking God for granted, as King Saul did, we should recall Saint Francis' words in the *Introduction to the Devout Life*, "It is not the consolations (*of God*) that we are to seek, but the Consoler."[17] With our focus truly upon the God who loves us, we can face any challenge with courage and honor.

MEDITATION: A SALESIAN METHOD

1. Remote Preparation

    a. Throw off all your concerns from the school day. *(Relax)*
    b. Read 1 Samuel 17:40-51.

When Goliath had sized David up, and seen that he was youthful... he held David in contempt... Then the Philistine cursed David by his gods.... David answered him: "You come against me with sword and spear, but I come against you in the name of the LORD of hosts .... all this multitude, too, shall learn that it is not by sword or spear that the LORD saves."The Philistine then moved to meet David at close quarters, while David ran quickly toward the battle line in the direction of the Philistine. David put his hand into the bag and took out a stone, hurled it with the sling, and struck the Philistine on the forehead. The stone embedded itself in his brow, and he fell prostrate on the ground.

*   Then David ran and stood over him; with the Philistine's own sword he dispatched him and cut off his head. When they saw that their hero was dead, the Philistines took to flight.*

2. Immediate Preparation

    a. Ask for a deeper awareness of God's presence.
    b. Ask for God's inspiration to pray sincerely.

3. Considerations *(Write down your insights about God's goodness.)*

    Imagine that you are young David facing the Philistine giant, Goliath. As you look upon the much larger Goliath and see the look of contempt in his eyes for your youth and size, how do you feel? What is it about God that gives you confidence that you can defeat this giant?

    Think about your anointing in Bethlehem by the prophet Samuel. Recall the words God used to explain to Samuel why you were chosen rather than your oldest brother Eliab in 1 Samuel 16:7.

    "Do not judge from his appearance or from his lofty stature, because I have rejected him. Not as man sees does God see, because man sees the appearance but the LORD looks into the heart."

    How is your acceptance of Goliath's challenge a sign that since Samuel's anointing you are truly filled with God's Spirit and destined to lead God's people as their next king?

48

As you run to battle, what prayer is going through your mind? How are your senses and breathing becoming more focused as you grab the smoothest stone from your bag to hurl at the giant?

You twirl the sling above your head. You know that you will probably get only one clean shot at Goliath before you are within his reach. As the stone releases from your sling, what are your thoughts? What prayer fills your heart?

As the stone strikes Goliath between the eyes and he falls towards you, what sounds do you hear? What emotions fill your heart? What words of praise to God come to mind?

4. Affections *(Write a three sentence spontaneous, heartfelt prayer.)*

What are you feeling as you see the Israelites regain their courage and their faith in God? What words could you use to humbly ask God for a greater spirit of courage *(as in the gift of Courage in the Sacrament of Confirmation)* in the midst of life's difficulties for God's greater glory?

5. Resolution *(Write a resolution that describes what you will do and when.)*

What do you feel you should do in order to live this day well in light of your meditation? Write one concrete resolution that can help you to gain courage while standing up for your faith in God.

6. TOP-Off *(Thanksgiving / Offering / Petition)*

a. Give thanksgiving to God for this experience of calm.

b. Offer to God your resolution of ....

c. Ask God to give you the grace to accomplish this.

7. Word Art *(Draw an image with words to help you recall your prayer time.)*

Pick any word, phrase or image from this meditation that can help you remember your time with God today. This word and/or image should also help you gratefully fulfill your resolution to become more courageous in standing up for your faith.

1. Remote Preparation Check Box ☐

2. Immediate Preparation Check Box ☐

3. Considerations *(Write down your insights about God and this story.)*

_____

_____

_____

_____

_____

_____

_____

_____

_____

_____

_____

_____

4. Affections *(Write a three sentence spontaneous, heartfelt prayer.)*

_____

_____

_____

_____

_____

_____

5. Resolution *(Write a resolution that describes what you will do and when.)*

_____

_____

_____

6. TOP-Off *(Thanksgiving / Offering / Petition)* **Check Box** ☐

7. Word Art *(Draw an image with words to help you recall your prayer time.)*

Solomon Builds the Temple

1 Kings 8:55-62

BEFORE WE BEGIN
Background Information

Have you ever wanted to do something special for someone else because he or she did something truly amazing for you? Maybe a teacher gave you the extra point you needed for an A and an exemption from the final exam. Maybe your parents surprised you by giving you the money for a school trip or a summer camp. No matter what it was, you were overcome with a spirit of gratitude.

This is what happened to Solomon who succeeded his father David as the king of Israel. King David had older sons who also sought to be king. Yet it was Solomon who was chosen over them. Immediately after becoming king, Solomon worried about how he could be a good king to so many people. Following his father David's advice to follow the ways of the Lord, Solomon asked for an understanding heart to judge the Israelite people and to learn right from wrong rather than asking God for even more wealth and power.

While it is always possible for us to forget to show the proper appreciation to God and others once our initial excitement passes, King Solomon followed through on his plan by building the Temple in Jerusalem and publicly leading Israel in its worship of God.

Salesian Concept
The Love of Benevolence

How do we respond to all the good things God has done for us? In the story of Joshua we were introduced to the Salesian concept of Love of Complacency. This happens when our love and appreciation for God grow in our hearts after we recognize God's goodness to us. The Love of Benevolence is our loving response to God's goodness. It bursts forth in loving actions from our hearts in order that others in the world may grow in their appreciation and love of God.

In the *Treatise on the Love of God* Saint Francis describes how benevolence grows out of complacency: "**Complacency draws the divine sweetness into our heart, ...with that it** (*our heart*) **is overcharged. But the love of benevolence makes our heart pass out of itself, and exhale itself...in all kinds of holy praises.**"[18] This is why the best act of benevolence we can offer God is our sincere worship at Mass that sets a good example for the young and gives hope to the old.

MEDITATION: A SALESIAN METHOD

1. Remote Preparation

   a. Throw off all your concerns from the school day. *(Relax)*
   b. Read 1 Kings 8:55-62.

Solomon stood and blessed the whole community of Israel, saying in a loud voice:, "Blessed be the LORD who has given rest to his people Israel, just as he promised. Not a single word has gone unfulfilled of the entire generous promise he made through his servant Moses. May the LORD, our God, be with us as he was with our fathers and may he not forsake us nor cast us off. May he draw our hearts to himself, that we may follow him in everything and keep the commands, statutes, and ordinances which he enjoined on our fathers. May this prayer I have offered to the LORD, our God, be present to him day and night, that he may uphold the cause of his servant and of his people Israel as each day requires, that all the peoples of the earth may know the LORD is God and there is no other. You must be wholly devoted to the LORD, our God, observing his statutes and keeping his commandments, as on this day." The king and all Israel with him offered sacrifices before the LORD.

2. Immediate Preparation

   a. Ask for a deeper awareness of God's presence.
   b. Ask for God's inspiration to pray sincerely.

3. Considerations *(Write down your insights about God's goodness.)*

   Imagine that you are King Solomon standing before the magnificent Temple. Recall all the good the Lord had done for Israel. Think about all the beauty of the Promised Land, God's eternal wisdom contained in the Law of Moses, and the peace and prosperity won by your father King David because his heart remained close to the Lord. Take time to remember that it took seven years for your people to build this marvelous structure. What are your wishes for the Temple? How can praises at the Temple serve as a sign to all peoples of the goodness of God? In the midst of hardship, how will people be comforted by God, who, though greater than the entire universe, still dwells with them?

Standing before all the people gathered in front of the Temple you recall what the Lord has done for you. Think about how you were chosen from all the other sons of David to be king, even though you did not have the military skill or power the others had. Why is it important that your gratitude towards God not end with the building of this Temple? How will you continue to thank God?

Think about the special gift of wisdom you were given by God. Recall how this wisdom has helped you grow in the eyes of the people as a good king and a capable ruler despite your young age. How necessary will it be to stay close to God in prayer in order to continue to grow in wisdom and understanding? How will you do it?

4. Affections *(Write a three sentence spontaneous, heartfelt prayer.)*

What are you feeling as you hear Solomon's prayer before the Temple? What can you say to God to pledge your gratitude for God's goodness and to help others appreciate God's goodness as well?

5. Resolution *(Write a resolution that describes what you will do and when.)*

What do you feel you should do in order to live this day well in light of your meditation? Write one concrete resolution that can help you act to make God's love grow more and more in the world.

6. TOP-Off *(Thanksgiving / Offering / Petition)*

a. Give thanksgiving to God for this experience of calm.

b. Offer to God your resolution of ....

c. Ask God to give you the grace to accomplish this.

7. Word Art *(Draw an image with words to help you recall your prayer time.)*

Pick any word, phrase or image from this meditation that can help you remember your time with God today. This word and/or image should also help you gratefully fulfill your resolution to show your love and appreciation of God to others.

1. Remote Preparation Check Box ☐

2. Immediate Preparation Check Box ☐

3. **Considerations** *(Write down your insights about God and this story.)*

_____

_____

_____

_____

_____

_____

_____

_____

_____

_____

_____

4. Affections *(Write a three sentence spontaneous, heartfelt prayer.)*

_____

_____

_____

_____

_____

_____

5. Resolution *(Write a resolution that describes what you will do and when.)*

_____

_____

_____

6. TOP-Off *(Thanksgiving / Offering / Petition)* **Check Box** ☐

7. Word Art *(Draw an image with words to help you recall your prayer time.)*

Israel's Wisdom Literature

Song of Songs 8:3-7

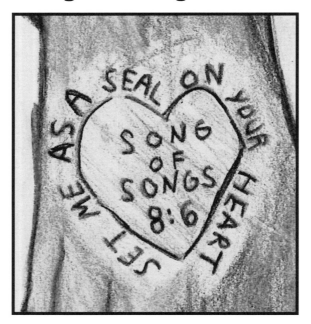

BEFORE WE BEGIN
Background Information

Do you like to eat? What is your favorite food? Maybe it is a cheese steak, lobster tail, burritos or moo-shu-pork. Have you ever wondered why God gave us the ability to experience all these different tastes? God could have created the world in such a way that we could get all the nutrition we need from tasteless water. Thank God for the variety of food we have as well as our taste buds and our sense of smell.

Do you like to sleep? God could have created humans in such a way that you would never need sleep. Think of all the extra homework teachers could assign if you did not need eight hours of sleep a night. Among other reasons God created sleep is so that we might have rest and renewal from our daily toils and struggles as well as a chance to begin each day with a fresh start.

The writer of the Song of Songs had the same awareness of the goodness of the experience of human love. The writer of the Song of Songs wrote a poetic play using the courtship or dating customs of his day to illustrate the goodness of human love. Prior to the writing of this love poetry, the prophets Isaiah, Jeremiah, and Ezekiel all used the image of a marital relationship to highlight the exclusive nature of God's covenant with the people of Israel.

Salesian Concept
Saint Francis de Sales: the Doctor of Divine Love

The Song of Songs was Saint Francis' favorite book from the Old Testament. Saint Francis often refers to the Song of Songs when illustrating our soul's quest for union with God in the *Treatise on the Love of God*.[19] In terms of our sexuality and chastity, Saint Francis highlights the goodness of sexual love, as the writer of the Song of Songs does, when it is truly grounded in the love of God.

In the *Introduction to the Devout Life* De Sales writes, **"You who wish to marry, jealously keep your first love for your future spouse. It is deceitful to offer (*your spouse*) a used, worn out, adulterated heart instead of a new and sincere one."**[20] As you meditate on the Song of Songs, think about how God designed human sexuality to bring us joy and happiness. Also pray that you are never deceived by the many cheap imitations of real marital love offered by our world today.

MEDITATION: A SALESIAN METHOD

1. Remote Preparation

a. Throw off all your concerns from the school day. *(Relax)*
b. Read Song of Songs 8:3-7.

The Bride: His left hand is under my head and his right arm embraces me. I adjure you, daughters of Jerusalem, by the gazelles and hinds of the field, do not arouse, do not stir up love, before its own time.

The Daughters of Jerusalem: Who is this coming up from the desert, leaning upon her lover?

The Groom: Under the apple tree I awakened you; it was there that your mother conceived you, it was there that your parent conceived.

The Bride: Set me as a seal on your heart, as a seal on your arm. For stern as death is love, relentless as the nether world is devotion; its flames are a blazing fire. Deep waters cannot quench love, nor floods sweep it away. Were one to offer all he owns to purchase love, he would be roundly mocked.

2. Immediate Preparation

a. Ask for a deeper awareness of God's presence.
b. Ask for God's inspiration to pray sincerely.

3. Considerations *(Write down your insights about God's goodness.)*

Imagine you are among the townspeople observing the Bride and the Groom as they are being watched and teased by those nosey daughters of Jerusalem. Why is everyone so interested in the two lovers? Is it because there is no other entertainment, or is it because everyone is seeking to learn what true love is like? Why does the Bride beg those Daughters of Jerusalem not to stir up love before its time?

Notice the admiring way the Bride speaks of the Groom. Is it not because she knows that her love is only for the Groom and his love is only for her?

You hear the Groom fondly recall the first time he met his Bride under the apple tree. What ideas fill your mind about the way love grows with time out of ordinary circumstances?

You hear the Bride ask her Groom to set her as a seal on his heart. What does this say about the exclusive nature of true marital love? How does this insight help you see that only a love committed to stand up to death and the flood of contrary emotions is worthy of marital love?

4. Affections *(Write a three sentence spontaneous, heartfelt prayer.)*

What are you feeling as these two souls express their true love for one another? How sincere is your wish to find someone to love with the true passion these two lovers share? What can you say to God to help you become an authentic, loving and lovable person, worthy of a true and passionate love that is stronger than death?

5. Resolution *(Write a resolution that describes what you will do and when.)*

What do you feel you should do in order to live this day well in light of your meditation? Write one concrete resolution that can help you become more loving and chaste in all your relationships.

6. TOP-Off *(Thanksgiving / Offering / Petition)*

a. Give thanksgiving to God for this experience of calm.
b. Offer to God your resolution of ....
c. Ask God to give you the grace to accomplish this.

7. Word Art *(Draw an image with words to help you recall your prayer time.)*

Pick any word, phrase or image from this meditation that can help you remember your time with God today. This word and/or image should also help you gratefully fulfill your resolution to love your future spouse with a passionate love that is stronger than death.

1. Remote Preparation Check Box ☐

2. Immediate Preparation Check Box ☐

3. **Considerations** *(Write down your insights about God and this story.)*

_____

_____

_____

_____

_____

_____

_____

_____

_____

_____

_____

_____

_____

4. Affections *(Write a three sentence spontaneous, heartfelt prayer.)*

_____

_____

_____

_____

_____

_____

5. Resolution *(Write a resolution that describes what you will do and when.)*

_____

_____

_____

6. TOP-Off *(Thanksgiving / Offering / Petition)* **Check Box** ☐

7. Word Art *(Draw an image with words to help you recall your prayer time.)*

Jeremiah's Temple Sermon

Jeremiah 7:4-5, 7-10

BEFORE WE BEGIN
Background Information

Have you ever had someone neglect an important aspect of his or her relationship with you? Perhaps that person gave you very expensive gifts but took no interest in what really mattered to you. You would be more upset if he or she always pledged to do better but never improved.

One of the ways the Israelites were called to express their love of God was through ritual sacrifices offered by a priest during their worship in the Temple. These animal sacrifices and bread offerings supported the priests who prayed for the needs of the people and preserved the terms of the covenant between God and Israel.

The problem began when many saw this ritual worship as the only necessary expression of their love for God. Prophets like Micah, Isaiah and Jeremiah continually warned that caring for the poor, widows and orphans was also essentially important to God. Yet consecutive generations failed to listen to these prophets and even took advantage of the poor to increase their wealth. Jeremiah warned that the Temple would not save them from the exile God threatened if the people continued to worship with insincere hearts.

We must admit as Catholics that we have not consistently worshipped God sincerely. Often our daily life does not reflect the promises we make during our worship at Mass. However, this can change if we prayerfully invite God into our daily life experience.

Salesian Concept
Making Good Resolutions after Prayer

Saint Francis de Sales warns us against living differently from the way we pray. In the *Introduction to the Devout Life* he wrote, "**It happens at times that people who consider themselves angels are hardly** (*even*) **good human beings, and there is often more grandeur** (*or goodness*) **in their words** (*in prayer*) **than in their sentiments** (*or attitudes*) **and their deeds.**"[21]

When Saint Francis taught, "**the Eucharist is the sun of all spiritual exercises,**"[22] he made it very clear that true holiness spreads beyond the Mass and reaches into every aspect of our lives. After praying we are to make a resolution "**to do ordinary things in an extraordinary way,**"[23] especially by offering to God all the good that we may do by saying **The Direction of Intention** found on page 110.

MEDITATION: A SALESIAN METHOD

1. Remote Preparation

> a. Throw off all your concerns from the school day. *(Relax)*
> b. Read Jeremiah7:1-5,7-10 below.

The following message came to Jeremiah from the LORD. "Stand at the gate of the house of the LORD, and there proclaim this message: Hear the word of the LORD, all you of Judah who enter these gates to worship the LORD!" Thus says the LORD of hosts, the God of Israel: "Reform your ways and your deeds, so that I may remain with you in this place. Put not your trust in the deceitful words: 'This is the temple of the LORD! The temple of the LORD! The temple of the LORD!'"

"Only if you thoroughly reform your deeds; if each of you deals justly with his neighbor; will I remain with you in this place, in the land which I gave your fathers long ago and forever. But here you are, putting your trust in deceitful words to your own loss!"

"Are you to steal and murder, commit adultery and perjury, burn incense to Baal, go after strange gods that you know not, and yet come to stand before me in this house which bears my name, and say: 'We are safe; we can commit all these abominations again?'"

2. Immediate Preparation

> a. Ask for a deeper awareness of God's presence.
> b. Ask for God's inspiration to pray sincerely.

3. Considerations *(Write down your insights about God's goodness.)*

Imagine that you are listening to Jeremiah on the steps leading into the Temple. As you hear him speak, you cannot help but wonder if Jeremiah is going to get in trouble opposing King Jehoiakim and his prophets who say that God would never allow his Temple to be destroyed. What do you think about Jeremiah's words against the king for taking God and His presence in the Temple for granted?

As you look at Jeremiah, there is nothing about him that makes you feel he can stand up to the power of the king. He is young, not that big or well built, and he seems a little sensitive and weak. Taking this into account, why do you think is he standing up against the king?

As Jeremiah continues you remember the old sanctuary in Shiloh that was established by Joshua up to the time of Samuel. You recall how it was destroyed by the Philistines because the priests there were greedy for the offerings of the people and did not respect God. What level of religious sincerity do you sense in your people?

As you hear the list of sins Jeremiah rattles off, you begin to realize that you are guilty of some of the same things yourself. What steps are you willing to take to make the changes that Jeremiah calls for in your life?

4. Affections *(Write a three sentence spontaneous, heartfelt prayer.)*

What are you feeling as you listen to Jeremiah calling you to worship and live with a sincere heart? What can you say to God to repent for not making his ways part of your day to day life? How can you pray to God to renew your heart that you may follow God's ways sincerely all the days of your life?

5. Resolution *(Write a resolution that describes what you will do and when.)*

What do you feel you should do in order to live this day well in light of your meditation? Write one concrete resolution that can serve as your response to repent for not worshipping and living sincerely.

6. TOP-Off *(Thanksgiving / Offering / Petition)*

a. Give thanksgiving to God for this experience of calm.

b. Offer to God your resolution of ....

c. Ask God to give you the grace to accomplish this.

7. Word Art *(Draw an image with words to help you recall your prayer time.)*

Pick any word, phrase or image from this meditation that can help you remember your time with God today. This word and/or image should also help you fulfill your resolution to live more in line with God's will so that your life reflects your worship of God.

1. Remote Preparation Check Box ☐

2. Immediate Preparation Check Box ☐

3. **Considerations** *(Write down your insights about God and this story.)*

_____

_____

_____

_____

_____

_____

_____

_____

_____

_____

_____

_____

_____

_____

4. Affections *(Write a three sentence spontaneous, heartfelt prayer.)*

_____

_____

_____

_____

_____

_____

5. Resolution *(Write a resolution that describes what you will do and when.)*

_____

_____

_____

_____

6. TOP-Off *(Thanksgiving / Offering / Petition)* **Check Box** ☐

7. Word Art *(Draw an image with words to help you recall your prayer time.)*

Ezra Reads the Law

Nehemiah 8:2-10

BEFORE WE BEGIN
Background Information

Have you ever realized that the way you were acting was causing problems for yourself and others? Maybe your group received a failing grade because all of you neglected directions for the project. Whatever it was, you would all like a second chance to do better.

This was the situation for the Jews who returned from the Babylonian Exile to rebuild Jerusalem and its Temple C.A. 535 B.C. As Ezra, the priestly scribe, and Nehemiah, the appointed governor, observed the behavior of the returning Jewish exiles, they noticed that they were guilty of the same types of sins against God and acts of injustice to the poor that led the people to be exiled to Babylon.

Ezra and Nehemiah knew that the people needed to be made aware of these faults to live faithfully with God before they renewed the covenant at the Temple. So Nehemiah gathered all the people and Ezra read the Law of Moses to them. When the people heard why their working on the Sabbath and charging interest on loans to the poor was so displeasing to God, they wept, fearing the worst. However, Ezra told them to rejoice in God's love and mercy instead.

Catholics are called to attend the Sacrament of Reconciliation after making a complete examination of conscience at least once a year. This may not seem like much fun, but it is the place where we can now experience God's merciful love in the face of our sinfulness.

Salesian Concept
The Protestation to Love God

In the first part of the *Introduction to the Devout Life* Saint Francis de Sales asks the reader to make a Protestation to Love God after making a general confession of one's sins based upon a detailed examination of conscience. De Sales taught that before we could fly in the way of devotion, we first needed to know and root out the bad habits and affection for sin that keeps us from fully loving God and others.

In the *Introduction to the Devout Life* Saint Francis gave penitents who confessed even the most serious sins some very optimistic advice: **"Never permit your heart to remain infected by sin for long, since you have such an easy remedy within reach."**[24] Of course, he meant the Sacrament of Reconciliation. De Sales is also quoted as saying, **"Instead of being discouraged by our imperfections, we should be consoled. If we know them, we can do something to correct them."**[25]

MEDITATION: A SALESIAN METHOD

1. Remote Preparation

a. Throw off all your concerns from the school day. *(Relax)*
b. Read Nehemiah 8:2-10 below.

On the first day of the seventh month, therefore, Ezra the priest brought the law before the assembly, which consisted of men, women, and those children old enough to understand. Standing at one end of the open place that was before the Water Gate, he read out of the book from daybreak till midday and all the people listened attentively to the book of the law.

Ezra opened the scroll so that all the people might see it; and, as he opened it, all the people rose. Then they bowed down and prostrated themselves before the LORD, their faces to the ground. Ezra read plainly from the book of the law of God, interpreting it so that all could understand what was read.

Then Nehemiah and Ezra the priest-scribe said to all the people: "Today is holy to the LORD your God. Do not be sad, and do not weep"-for all the people were weeping as they heard the words of the law. Ezra said further: "Go, eat rich foods and drink sweet drinks, and allot portions to those who had nothing prepared; for today is holy to our LORD. Do not be saddened this day, for rejoicing in the LORD must be your strength!"

2. Immediate Preparation

a. Ask for a deeper awareness of God's presence.
b. Ask for God's inspiration to pray sincerely.

3. Considerations *(Write down your insights about God's goodness.)*

Imagine that you are there with all the returning exiles at the Water Gate as Ezra reads from the Law of Moses. Think about how happy you are to be back in Jerusalem but also how difficult it has been to establish your household and work on building the Temple at the same time. Why is it important for you to renew the covenant?

Think of the Jews who did not return to Jerusalem. Why do you wish they were here with you at the Temple on this great day? How will reestablishing the worship in the Temple of Jerusalem help unify your people and serve as a sign for other Jews to return home?

As Ezra reads from the Law of Moses, you recall that it was disobedience to the laws of faithful worship and just living that caused the Exile in the first place. How have you been guilty of ignoring God's will in the midst of your busy life?

As people around you begin to weep for their unfaithfulness to the covenant, what surprises you about Ezra's call to "eat rich foods and drink sweet drinks?" How have Ezra's words "do not be saddened this day, for rejoicing in the LORD must be your strength," renewed your desire to serve God? What difference will this make in your worship of God and in your actions on behalf of the poor?

4. Affections *(Write a three sentence spontaneous, heartfelt prayer.)*

What are you feeling as Ezra consoles the returning exiles? What can you say in gratitude to God for the gift of his forgiveness? What acts of unfaithfulness do you want to confess to God? What words best express your desire to love and serve God with your whole heart?

5. Resolution *(Write a resolution that describes what you will do and when.)*

What do you feel you should do in order to live this day well in light of your meditation? Write one concrete resolution that can serve as your response to rededicate yourself to loving and serving God.

6. TOP-Off *(Thanksgiving / Offering / Petition)*

a. Give thanksgiving to God for this experience of calm.

b. Offer to God your resolution of ....

c. Ask God to give you the grace to accomplish this.

7. Word Art *(Draw an image with words to help you recall your prayer time.)*

Pick any word, phrase or image from this meditation that can help you remember your time with God today. This word and/or image should also help you fulfill your resolution to root out anything that gets in the way of your faithfully loving and serving God and others.

1. Remote Preparation Check Box ☐

2. Immediate Preparation Check Box ☐

3. Considerations *(Write down your insights about God and this story.)*

_____

_____

_____

_____

_____

_____

_____

_____

_____

_____

_____

_____

4. Affections *(Write a three sentence spontaneous, heartfelt prayer.)*

_____

_____

_____

_____

_____

_____

5. Resolution *(Write a resolution that describes what you will do and when.)*

_____

_____

_____

6. TOP-Off *(Thanksgiving / Offering / Petition)* **Check Box** ☐

7. Word Art *(Draw an image with words to help you recall your prayer time.)*

The Fiery Furnace

Daniel 3:88-93

"Bless the LORD; praise and exalt Him above all forever."
Daniel 3:88

BEFORE WE BEGIN
Background Information

Have you ever been in a no win situation? Maybe an adversary in a personal conflict or in an athletic contest had such a huge advantage that only an act of God could overcome it. All you could do was stand up for yourself, do what was right and take what was coming.

This is what the Jews faced after they were freed from the Babylonian Exile during the time of Alexander the Great C.A. 333 B.C. His Greeks conquered most of the known world and forced every nation to adopt Greek culture and religion or face death. The First and Second Books of Maccabees reflect the religious zeal of Jews who would rather fight and even die to keep the Jewish Law than abandon it.

The prophet Daniel used apocalyptic writing to send a different message. He wrote during the brutal reign of Antiochus Epiphanes IV C.A. 167-164 B.C. He told Jews to practice non-violent resistance and risk martyrdom by practicing their outlawed faith in this apparent no -win situation. The prophet Daniel urged the Jews of his day to trust that God, the Lord of History, would save them if they died for their faith.

As Catholics, even though we have Jesus' Resurrection to help us, it can still be difficult to trust in God's power to save us in our biggest trials. Let us pray for greater trust in God's plan to save us.

Salesian Concept
Trust in God's Providence

As a missionary in the Calvinist region called the Chablais, Saint Francis de Sales risked his life on many occasions. Not only were there attempts on his life, but he also faced danger from wild animals and the elements of nature. An amazing story of Saint Francis' trust in God is told in Elizabeth Stopp's book *Saint Francis de Sales: A Testimony by Saint Chantal.* While in a small boat during a fierce storm on Lake Geneva, Saint Francis was actually thrilled to have his life so dependent on God's providence rather than being frightened by it.[26]

Saint Francis' thoughts about death are recorded in the *Golden Counsels,* **"The words: 'We must die' are harsh, but they are followed by words of great sweetness: 'in order to be united with God through death.'"**[27]

MEDITATION: A SALESIAN METHOD

1. Remote Preparation

a. Throw off all your concerns from the school day. *(Relax)*
b. Read Daniel 3:88-93 below.

(Three young men sang from the fiery furnace.) ". . . Bless the Lord; praise and exalt him above all forever. For he has delivered us from the nether world, and saved us from the power of death. He has freed us from the raging flame and delivered us from the fire. Give thanks to the Lord, for he is good, for his mercy endures forever. Bless the God of gods, all you who fear the Lord; praise him and give him thanks, because his mercy endures forever." Hearing them sing, and astonished at seeing them alive, King Nebuchadnezzar rose in haste and asked his nobles, "Did we not cast three men bound into the fire?" "Assuredly, O king," they answered. "But," he replied, "I see four men unfettered and unhurt, walking in the fire, and the fourth looks like a son of God." Then Nebuchadnezzar came to the opening of the white-hot furnace and called to Shadrach, Meshach, and Abednego: "Servants of the Most High God come out." Thereupon Shadrach, Meshach, and Abednego came out of the fire.

2. Immediate Preparation

a. Ask for a deeper awareness of God's presence.
b. Ask for God's inspiration to pray sincerely.

3. Considerations *(Write down your insights about God's goodness.)*

Imagine that you are watching as Shadrach, Meshach and Abednego are summoned before King Nebuchadnezzar for refusing to bow down and worship the golden statue the king erected. With all the government officials standing by, these three young men remained calm in the face of the king's anger as well as the threat of being thrown into the white hot fiery furnace. What are the expressions on the faces of King Nebuchadnezzar, the three young men and of all the government officials who are watching?

As the three young men are thrown into the furnace, you hear joyful singing rather than screams of torment and pain. When the king looks into the furnace, he is further surprised to see a fourth person, an angel of the Lord, driving out the flames of the white hot furnace. The more the king's men stoke the fire, the more the angel fans the flames out of the furnace leaving Shadrach, Meshach and Abednego unharmed. How do the king and people react to these surprises?

As you watch the three young men being let out of the fiery furnace, what is the reaction of everyone there? What can you take from their example in terms of courage and trust in God for your life?

4. Affections *(Write a three sentence spontaneous, heartfelt prayer.)*

What are you feeling as Shadrach, Meshach and Abednego are being led out of the fiery furnace unharmed? What are your feelings about having to suffer for doing God's Will? What can you say to God to show your trust in his saving power? What praise can you offer God?

5. Resolution *(Write a resolution that describes what you will do and when.)*

What do you feel you should do in order to live this day well in light of your meditation? Write one concrete resolution that can serve as your response to trust in God's saving and providential care.

6. TOP-Off *(Thanksgiving / Offering / Petition)*
a. Give thanksgiving to God for this experience of calm.
b. Offer to God your resolution of ....
c. Ask God to give you the grace to accomplish this.

7. Word Art *(Draw an image with words to help you recall your prayer time.)*

Pick any word, phrase or image from this meditation that can help you remember your time with God today. This word and/or image should also help you fulfill your resolution to remember that trusting God is better than taking the easy way out, even in difficult times.

1. Remote Preparation Check Box ☐

2. Immediate Preparation Check Box ☐

3. **Considerations** *(Write down your insights about God and this story.)*

_____

_____

_____

_____

_____

_____

_____

_____

_____

_____

_____

_____

_____

4. Affections *(Write a three sentence spontaneous, heartfelt prayer.)*

_____

_____

_____

_____

_____

_____

5. Resolution *(Write a resolution that describes what you will do and when.)*

_____

_____

_____

6. TOP-Off *(Thanksgiving / Offering / Petition)* **Check Box** ☐

7. Word Art *(Draw an image with words to help you recall your prayer time.)*

Micah's Prophecy on the Messiah

Micah 5:1-3

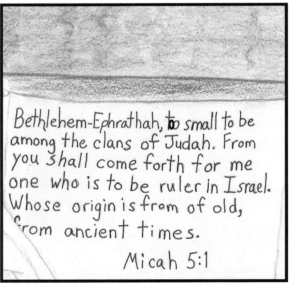

Bethlehem-Ephrathah, to small to be among the clans of Judah. From you shall come forth for me one who is to be ruler in Israel. Whose origin is from of old, from ancient times.

Micah 5:1

BEFORE WE BEGIN

Background Information

People have been shell shocked during our recent economic meltdown. Many of our national problems have come from the sins of pride and greed that went unchecked in our political, social and economic lives. Hindsight shows our bad choices made it impossible to avoid these negative consequences. The question is, "Can we change course soon enough to limit the damage these flaws have caused?"

The prophet Micah warned that God would have to give a sinful Israel up to foreign powers. This happened during the Assyrian and Babylonian Exiles. These hardships would help the Chosen People come to their senses and change their course from injustice to justice and from empty worship to heartfelt worship and praise of God.

However, Micah also promised that God would renew Israel's standing in the world by sending a gentle and humble Messiah to shepherd God's people Israel and bring peace to the ends of the earth. Micah's prophesy renewed their hope in God's salvation as they suffered under the weight of Rome and their PAX Romano.

The question for us is: "Can we turn to God for help in our personal and national difficulties, or will we continue to seek solutions that leave God and his saving grace out of the picture?"

Salesian Concept
The Salesian Virtues: Gentleness and Humility

Saint Francis de Sales' favorite image of Jesus was the Gentle and Humble Jesus from Matthew 11:29. This is why Salesians are called to practice the virtues of Gentleness and Humility as we seek to "**Live Jesus.**" De Sales firmly believed that God's ways are wiser than human practices unaided by God's grace and revealed truth. Who could have imagined that sin and death could be overcome by a poor and humble infant born of a gentle virgin named Mary?

Saint Francis knew the power of gentleness and humility from the example of Jesus, the Prince of Peace. De Sales explained the true nature of humility in the *Introduction to the Devout Life;* "**In choosing which virtues to practice, we ought to prefer those that are most appropriate to our duties of state, than those** (*virtues*) **that are more to our taste.**"[28] With regard to the power of gentleness, he is often quoted: "**Nothing is as strong as true gentleness, and nothing is as gentle as true strength.**"[29]

MEDITATION: A SALESIAN METHOD

1. Remote Preparation

    a. Throw off all your concerns from the school day. *(Relax)*
    b. Read Micah 5:1-3 below.

But you, Bethlehem-Ephrathah too small to be among the clans of Judah, From you shall come forth for me one who is to be ruler in Israel; Whose origin is from of old, from ancient times.

(Therefore the Lord will give them up, until the time when she who is to give birth has borne, and the rest of his brethren shall return to the children of Israel.)

He shall stand firm and shepherd his flock by the strength of the LORD, in the majestic name of the LORD, his God; and they shall remain, for now his greatness shall reach to the ends of the earth; he shall be peace.

2. Immediate Preparation

    a. Ask for a deeper awareness of God's presence.
    b. Ask for God's inspiration to pray sincerely.

3. Considerations *(Write down your insights about God's goodness.)*

    Imagine that you are reading Micah's prophecy with Mary and Joseph just before they were required to travel to Bethlehem as part of the census ordered by Rome C.A. 6 B.C. The Romans have acted cruelly towards your people. They have corrupted your Jewish leaders. While it appears that King Herod is responding to Jewish concerns by refurnishing the Temple in Jerusalem, all of Israel's wealth is leaving the country in the form of heavy taxes paid to Rome. How hopeful are you that this prophecy will be fulfilled in your lifetime?

    As you read about the promise of a ruler from Bethlehem-Ephrathah, the small village of King David's birth, which qualities of King David would you like to see in the long awaited Messiah?

You think of all the religious political groups claiming to speak for God. There are the Herodians, who cooperate with the Roman occupation so it will be less bloody. Opposing them are the Zealots, who believe the only good Roman is a dead Roman. There are also the Essenes, priests living in the desert waiting to fight a holy war. Then there are the Sadduccees, who serve as priests and Levites in the Temple. Last are the Pharisees, the rabbis who teach in the local synagogues. These last two groups disagree on everything from the Law of Moses to the possibility of a resurrection for the faithful. How does the situation call for a firm and strong ruler from God who will also be a gentle and humble shepherd of God's people? What will it take for this Messiah to bring peace to your land and the world?

4. Affections *(Write a three sentence spontaneous, heartfelt prayer.)*

What are you feeling as you read God's promise to save Israel from its foes by one coming from the humble town of Bethlehem-Ephrathah? What can you say to God to be more accepting of his help from unexpected places? What are your feelings about God's plan to save us all from sin and death?

5. Resolution *(Write a resolution that describes what you will do and when.)*

What do you feel you should do in order to live this day well in light of your meditation? Write one concrete resolution that can serve as your response to accept God's help and God's plan in your life.

6. TOP-Off *(Thanksgiving / Offering / Petition)*
a. Give thanksgiving to God for this experience of calm.
b. Offer to God your resolution of ....
c. Ask God to give you the grace to accomplish this.

7. Word Art *(Draw an image with words to help you recall your prayer time.)*

Pick any word, phrase or image from this meditation that can help you remember your time with God today. This word and/or image should also help you humbly accept God's gentle help to guide you in the most difficult times in your life.

1. Remote Preparation Check Box ☐

2. Immediate Preparation Check Box ☐

3. Considerations *(Write down your insights about God and this story.)*

_____

_____

_____

_____

_____

_____

_____

_____

_____

_____

_____

_____

4. Affections *(Write a three sentence spontaneous, heartfelt prayer.)*

_____

_____

_____

_____

_____

_____

5. Resolution *(Write a resolution that describes what you will do and when.)*

_____

_____

_____

6. TOP-Off *(Thanksgiving / Offering / Petition)* **Check Box** ☐

7. Word Art *(Draw an image with words to help you recall your prayer time.)*

Introduction to Iconic Lectio by Neil Kane

In the previous pages you have been practicing Lectio Divina or sacred reading of the Word. Now it's time to introduce the practice of Iconic Lectio or sacred reading of an icon or image.

In the Christian Churches of the East, where iconography began, one is said to "write," not paint, a sacred icon. The idea that God communicates or reveals himself through the Word made flesh, led to the creation of the icons. Therefore, we can now practice Iconic Lectio by discerning the meaning of an image or icon.

This book takes the sacred iconic tradition from the Byzantine or Eastern Church and alters it slightly to fit our modern times. We read the meaning of a visual icon or image by contemplating it. We experience and seek to understand the significance of colors in the drawing. While beholding the facial expressions of ancient biblical figures like Moses or David, we can enter more deeply into their experience as well as the mood, the tone, the feeling of the icon.

The goal is to appreciate the icon rather than to intellectually dissect it. Iconic Lectio should use the senses, heart and the mind. While Lectio Divina uses the imagination to awaken our thoughts and feelings, Iconic Lectio uses our senses to enliven one's mind and heart.

Under each of the pictures you will find two questions to help you enter into the mood, tone and feeling of the icon as well as your own personal awareness of God's activity in your life. Do not feel limited by these questions, as the Holy Spirit may lead you to consider other aspects of the image for your own spiritual welfare. The goal is to come away from your prayerful experience with a new and profound sense of God's presence and love in your life that you can take with you. Therefore, in group discussions you can feel free to share your thoughts as long as you are viewing the same icon everyone else is. Each icon offers many different starting points for meditation. While it is important to keep to some traditional rules of faith, like the Trinity is the Father, Son and Holy Spirit, we do no service by painting God into a confining box based upon one's past experience.

Finally, you may wish to draw your own icons that serve as a reminder and marker of your spiritual growth. You do not need to be an artist to do this. See the Word Art example on page 110 for John 14:6 where Jesus says, "I am the way, the truth and the life."

All Icons are doors to the Sacred.

David Writes Psalm 119
How does this image show prayer can grow in times spent alone?
How do you pray when you are alone with God?

Genesis 1 The Priestly Creation Story
Find one symbol for each person of the Trinity in this image.
What goodness in the Trinity do you see reflected in the human family?

Genesis 12 The Call of Abram
Do you see the 3 stars referring to Abram's descendants?
How is God calling you to have faith in your future?

Genesis 21 The Birth of Isaac
Name 3 adjectives that describe Abraham and Sarah in this image that
should describe all people of faith?
What three adjectives would best describe your life of faith?

Genesis 45 Joseph in Egypt
Can you name the 8 stories of Joseph depicted in this image?
What good has come out of your most difficult times?

Exodus 3 The Call of Moses
What do you think Moses is thinking about in this image?
How do you feel when God calls you to help those treated unfairly?

Joshua 24 The Israelites Enter the Promised Land
Which of the events of the Exodus do you think of the most?
In what ways does your family serve the Lord and keep the Commandments?

1Samuel 17 David Defeats Goliath
What do you see in David's face that shows his trust in God's help?
What special task is God strengthening you to do?

1 Kings 8 Solomon Builds the Temple
What does this image of Solomon show about the nature of prayer?
How often do you pray to God and for what do you pray?

Song of Songs 8:6
How does this image reflect the goodness of God's gift of human love?
Do your relationships with the opposite sex reflect this same image?

Jeremiah 7 The Temple Sermon
What do the faces tell you about the reactions to Jeremiah's words?
In what ways do you need to reform your life to faithfully follow God?

Nehemiah 3 Ezra Reads the Law
How do these words of Ezra console the returning Exiles?
How do you view God, as a strict judge or a loving father?

Daniel 3 The Fiery Furnace
How do these young men demonstrate trust in God in the face of death?
How would you respond to God if you were facing your own death?

Micah 3 The Messiah
What do you feel Mary and Joseph are thinking of in this scene?
How much faith do you place in God's plan for your eternal happiness?

95

Appendix Section

**An Introduction to the Life of Saint Francis de Sales
and Salesian Prayer and Spirituality**

Based upon *Praying with Francis de Sales*
by Rev. Thomas F. Dailey, OSFS.

Stained glass window images courtesy of
Rev. Robert McGilvary, OSFS

The Birth and Times of Saint Francis de Sales

Saint Francis de Sales was born on August 21, 1567, in the Chateau de Sales near Annecy, France. The oldest son of Francois and Francoise de Sales, Francis grew up around the beauty of the French Alps and the peacefulness of Lake Annecy. The goodness of God's creation helped a young Saint Francis de Sales look for and see all the goodness around him and find God.

Francis grew up during the historical time of the Renaissance and the Reformation in the Duchy of Savoy. The Renaissance was a time of a rebirth of learning due to the rediscovery of Greek and Roman literature and philosophy, as well as ancient scientific and architectural wonders. The Renaissance was also marked by the discovery of the New World of the Americas and the invention of the printing press. These developments changed the way people saw the world and led people to question many of the most foundational aspects of life.

Name icons of the Renaissance.

The Protestant Reformation was carried along by this spirit of change and in the growing self-awareness of nationalism. For the first time, people were seeking to identify themselves by their national origin rather than their religious identity. The idea of Christendom in the Middle Ages was now being replaced by nationalism. The idea of all Christians being united under the successors of Saint Peter in Rome, was now seen as German, Swiss, English and French-speaking Christians being forced to obey a foreign Italian Pope.

Francis' parents sought to prepare him to become a leader in times filled with both promise and challenge. In order to live up to his potential, Francis was trained to practice true civility as a gentleman. Civility is the awareness and intention of being genuinely good to one another by relating to others in respectful, just, and loving ways.[30] In this section you will see how Saint Francis practiced this important skill and became know as the Gentleman Saint.

Application for Today

1) What major events in our recent history have shaped the spirit of our time the most?

2) In what areas of life do we most need civility today? Why?

97

Humanistic Education

Saint Francis was encouraged to grow in both love of God and love of learning. He was tutored by a Jesuit priest named Father Déage. His studies focused upon the French language, the classic stories from Greece and Rome, reasoning and debating skills, and religion. It is no wonder that Saint Francis would call knowledge the Eighth Sacrament.

Given all this knowledge and strengthened by God's love, Saint Francis learned that we are all able to make a new and better world by living a life of true devotion.[31] Devotion is true love of God. It leads us not only to do God's Will, but also to do it promptly, carefully and often. As a result, Saint Francis took to heart the lessons in prayer he received from Father Déage. Saint Francis learned how to use his imagination to feel the constant presence and love of God. He began to use prayer to become his very best at home and at school as well as to be his best socially, morally and athletically.

Just like you Saint Francis had a life beyond the classroom. He was also a skilled athlete, mastering horseback riding and swordsmanship, which were the most prized athletic talents of his time. He even knew all the social dances of his day. With the proper balance of faith and reason, Francis not only succeeded at many different activities, but he also learned how to find God's presence in everything he was doing. It is with this goal in mind that Saint Francis de Sales would later teach people to say the Direction of Intention. See page 110. Saint Francis saw this prayer as a way to 1) remember God's presence, 2) offer God all the good that we may do and 3) accept any difficulties we might experience in life.

Young Francis prays the Memorare.

Francis was not free of spiritual difficulties, even though he had a priest for a tutor. In Paris, he suffered a spiritual crisis after hearing lectures on Predestination, the false belief that some people are destined for hell. The lectures confused him so much that he questioned whether he would ever get into heaven. After praying the Memorare, Francis decided to depend solely upon God's great love no matter what happened in life.[31]

Application for Today

1) What difficulties do young people face in their spiritual lives?

2) What advice would you give for any of these difficulties?

The Priest-Missionary

At the age of 26, Saint Francis de Sales returned home from the prestigious University of Padua in Italy. He earned a degree in Civil Law to remain faithful to his father's wishes to become a lawyer and to the Signified Will of God by keeping the Fourth Commandment, "Honor your father and mother." Yet, Francis also studied Church Law at Padua, and now as an adult, he announced his intention to become a priest. Francis was ordained on December 18, 1593. His first priestly assignment was to restore Catholicism in the Chablais region in Switzerland which was a stronghold of Calvinism. This was a very difficult and dangerous task. Francis faced threats on his life as well as the brutal elements of nature.

Francis de Sales travels to defend the Catholic faith in the Chablais.

Francis engaged the people on their own terms and slowly but surely through gentleness and humility was able to lead them to reconsider their Calvinist beliefs. The secret of Francis' missionary success was his willingness to dialogue with everyone in a peaceful pursuit of truth that recognized the goodness of all people rather than the validity of every idea.

Francis wrote a series of apologetic pamphlets to start conversations with fallen away Catholics and to win them back to the practice of their Catholic faith. In these pamphlets Francis clearly made use of his legal training by setting forth logical arguments as to why Catholicism, and not Calvinism, was the true faith handed down from the Apostles. These pamphlets were later published in a book called the *Catholic Controversy.*[32]

Application for Today

1) What aspects of Saint Francis' missionary style would be effective in today's pluralistic world?

2) Write an explanation of an aspect of Catholic faith under attack today that you believe Saint Francis would seek to defend.

The Bishop of Geneva

After winning so many people back to the practice of their original Catholic faith, Francis was consecrated as the Bishop of Geneva. However, Francis de Sales moved the Cathedral to Annecy, France, for the safety and welfare of the people he led back to the Catholic faith.

With all the confusion over the truth of religion caused by the Reformation, one of Francis's most important tasks as bishop was to help the people understand the teachings of the Council of Trent (1545-1563). This Council reaffirmed the traditional teachings of the Church in response to the Reformation. It called for better religious education of all the faithful through the use of a standard catechism or book of religious truths.

Application for Today

1) What Vatican II teachings are Catholic bishops trying to promote today?

2) Look up your bishop's schedule on your diocesan website. What issues have bishops spoken on lately?

In true Salesian humility, even as a bishop, Francis personally taught catechism or CCD classes. Francis also invented a type of sign language to teach catechism to a deaf boy, whom no one else wanted or was able to teach. It is because of this that Saint Francis de Sales was named the Patron Saint of the Deaf.

In true Salesian gentleness, Francis emphasized personal contact with the people in his care, commoner and scholar alike. Francis also started the practice of parish visitations where he would travel to every parish church in his diocese. Later Francis de Sales co-founded the Florimontane Academy where humanistic scholars could engage in discussions to develop human knowledge. The Florimontane Academy highlighted a major Catholic belief that faith and reason are both gifts from God that help us know God more fully. Remember that Saint Francis called knowledge the Eighth Sacrament.[33]

Francis de Sales listening to scholars at the Florimontane Academy.

The Spiritual Director

As a bishop Francis traveled throughout France, Switzerland, and Italy. In his journeys, he met many people, like Jane de Chantal, who would help Francis develop and promote what we know today as Salesian Spirituality. Because of the uniquely simple and practical manner in which Francis de Sales preached, he was sought after for spiritual counsel or advice.

Francis de Sales wrote thousands of letters of spiritual advice, primarily in the mornings due to his hectic schedule. He wrote to religious orders, well-to-do nobles, and even simple field laborers on how to find God in the midst of daily tasks.

Eventually Francis became the spiritual director for Jane de Chantal, a young widow with four children. They met for the first time while Francis was giving Lenten sermons in Dijon, France, in 1604. Their spiritual friendship would blossom into what is known as Salesian Spirituality.[33]

Francis meets Jane in Dijon, France, during the Lenten Sermons of 1604.

Saint Francis' spiritual advice is often characterized as "inspired common sense" such as his saying, "One Our Father said with devotion is better than one hundred said quickly and hurriedly,"[34] or "True devotion (*holiness*) hinders no one. Rather it perfects everything. Whenever it is out of keeping with any person's calling, it must be false."[35] Some signature aspects of his practical optimistic spiritual advice are as follows:

1) Take a practical view concerning holiness.

2) Find God by being focused upon the positive.

3) Love God in what one is doing at the "present moment."

4) Build spiritual friendships where the focus is on loving God more and more.[36]

Application for Today

1) Why do you think that the time is right for spiritual advice that is both practical and optimistic?

2) Which of the four aspects of Salesian spiritual advice is the most useful to you? How can you practice it in your life today?

The Spiritual Writer

Francis' popularity as a teacher of spiritual truths led his friends to persuade him to publish longer books on the subject of Christian life in the world.[36] The *Introduction to the Devout Life* and the *Treatise on the Love of God* are his most popular books.

The *Introduction to the Devout Life* (1609) was addressed to a fictional woman named "Philothea." Philothea means "a soul in love with God." The *Introduction to the Devout Life* is the forerunner of the Vatican II teaching, "the universal call to holiness." It was based upon Jesuit spiritual exercises. In the *Introduction*, Francis uses imaginative meditations, often focusing upon the affections of one's heart, leading the reader to make a resolution to lead a devout life.

The *Introduction to the Devout Life* covers the following:

Part One: True Devotion
Part Two: Prayer and the Sacraments
Part Three: The Practice of Virtue
Part Four: The Struggle against Temptations
Part Five: Renewing One's Desire to Lead a Devout Life.

The *Treatise on the Love of God* (1616) is addressed to a fictional character named Theotimus which means "a lover of God." In the *Treatise* Francis spells out how to unite our will to the will of God so as to advance further in the love of God. Francis' writing is based upon sound philosophy and psychology, with examples from nature, the Bible, as well as the lives of the saints.

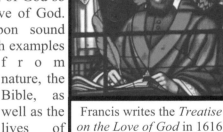

Francis writes the *Treatise on the Love of God* in 1616.

In the *Introduction* Francis shows how all people could live a life of holiness. In the *Treatise* Francis illustrates how the profound mysteries of God's love can be found by practicing little virtues everyday .[37]

Application for Today

1) What do you think makes a person truly holy in today's world? Give examples.

2) Right now, which part of the *Introduction* would be of the most interest for you to study? Why?

3) Why is uniting our will to God's will the truest sign of our love of God?

The Founding Father

During Francis' time, people falsely believed that only those who withdrew from the world to pray and follow strict religious disciplines could be truly holy. In 1610 Francis and Jane founded the Visitation Sisters of Holy Mary. The new order was founded upon charity rather than the traditional religious vows of poverty, chastity and obedience. Francis wrote in the Book of Professions, "We have no bond but the bond of love." Francis also gave the sisters the *Spiritual Directory* that explained how to find God in every daily activity from waking up to eating, to waking up in the middle of the night. Rather than focusing upon rigorous practices of self-denial, these sisters would go out to visit and care for the sick.

The Visitation Sisters receive the Spiritual Directory from Saint Francis.

Thus older women, widows, or even the disabled who were not strong enough to enter traditional religious life found a home with the Visitation or Visitandine sisters.

Later Francis and Jane were told that they would receive approval from the Pope only if their Visitandine Order remained in a cloister.39 Saint Francis and Saint Jane accepted the news from the Vatican with typical Salesian gentleness and humility.38

It was a blessing that the Visitation Sisters were kept from going out into the homes of the sick and poor. Had their original ministry been approved, they may have had little time to preserve for us the vast treasury of spiritual wisdom of Saint Francis de Sales and Saint Jane de Chantal. Later their spiritual friends Saint Vincent de Paul and Saint Louise de Marillac founded the Daughters of Charity to care for the poor and sick.

Application for Today

1) Look up Luke 1:39-56 in your Bible. Why do you think that Saint Francis and Saint Jane chose to name their order the Visitation Sisters of Holy Mary?

2) How did Saint Francis and Saint Jane live by their teachings about true gentleness and humility? How can we do the same today?

The Saintly Patron

Francis journeyed all through France to preach and to attend to the growing number of Visitation monasteries. While traveling with both the King of France and the Duke of Savoy, Francis declined their offer to dine and lodge in grand style in favor of staying with his Visitation Sisters in nearby Lyon. Later during that visit Francis de Sales died of a stroke on December 28, 1622.

Francis and Jane: founders of Salesian Spirituality.

It did not take long for Francis de Sales to be named a saint. He was canonized by Pope Alexander VII in 1665. You can read Saint Francis' life of holiness in *St Francis de Sales: A Testimony by St Chantal* by Elizabeth Stopp. His Feast Day is **January 24**.

Pope Pius IX declared him Patron Saint of the Deaf in 1854. Pope Pius XI declared Francis the Patron of Journalists and of the Catholic Press. Pope Pius IX also declared him a Doctor of the Church in 1877, which means that not one spiritual error was found in all his writings.39 Besides being the patron of religious orders like the Oblates of Saint Francis de Sales, the Oblate Sisters of Saint Francis de Sales and the Visitation Sisters of Holy Mary, Saint Francis de Sales is also the patron of many dioceses throughout the world.

Application for Today

1) What does Saint Francis de Sales, as one of only 33 Doctors in the 2000 year history of the Church, say about the reliability of Salesian Spirituality?

Saint Francis de Sales Data

Born: August 21, 1567

Education: Clermont School (Paris)
University of Padua (Italy)

Career: Bishop of Geneva
Co- Founder of the Visitation
Sisters of Holy Mary.

Motto or Saying: Live Jesus!

Favorite Bible Passage: Matthew 11:29

Salesian Imagination: Seek the Possibilities

Saint Francis de Sales saw the goodness of God and its reflection in all creation as the starting point for all theology. In fact, Saint Francis de Sales used over 33,000 images in his writings to help people better understand and appreciate the beauty of their Catholic faith.

Saint Francis de Sales encourages us to imagine Christ's great love for all.

At a young age Francis was introduced to the use of imagination in prayer through his tutor, Father Déage. However, Francis would later develop these imaginative techniques in a new way. The main focus of Salesian meditation is to use the power of our imagination to discover the constant presence of God in our lives.[40]

In the Salesian tradition imagination is not fantasy but seeing what is often overlooked and not taken advantage of in life. Imagination in this sense is like people who think outside the box for a solution or people who can recognize the presence of goodness in themselves and others where pessimistic people fail.

In the next few pages and throughout this book you will be led through imaginative meditative exercises. Place yourself in these stories with God and consider his goodness in them so that you may see God's activity more clearly in your present life experience. This prayerful exercise is called Lectio Divina. It is an ancient form of Christian prayer that Pope Benedict XVI and many bishops of the United States are now promoting. See page 2 for direct quotes from the Pope and Bishops.

Application for Today

1) Compare Francis' use of imagination to athletes or public speakers who use visualization techniques to succeed.

2) What areas of your spiritual life could benefit from these helpful imaginative visualization methods?

Salesian Prayer: Union of Hearts

In our scientific age we know that the heart pumps blood and oxygen throughout our bodies, but at the same time we all recognize the heart as the imaginative physical symbol for a person's soul and spirit.

It was the humble and gentle heart of Jesus in Matthew 11:25-32 that Saint Francis de Sales chose for his primary image of Jesus.

It should be no surprise that the heart is seen as the central location for our spiritual journey towards God and that Salesian Spirituality views prayer as a "union of hearts"; that is, our heart with the Sacred Heart of Jesus.

The Salesian image of prayer is a union of hearts, our heart linked with the Sacred Heart of Jesus.

In Matthew 6:21 Jesus said, "For where your treasure is, there also will your heart be." Saint Francis taught that if we truly love God, then we will not only seek out God's presence in the world (*Complacence*), but we will also seek to make God's goodness known and praised throughout the world (*Benevolence*).[41] Later you will be asked to write your own spontaneous prayers to express how your love and affection for God have grown based upon your insights from your meditations.

The Treatise on the Love of God Book V. Chapter 9.
Benevolence Makes Us Call All Creatures To The Praise Of God.

"The heart that is taken and pressed with a desire of praising the divine goodness more than it is able, after many endeavors goes oftentimes out of itself, to invite all creatures to help it in its design.... Complacency draws the Divine sweetness into our hearts, which so ardently fills itself there with that it is overcharged. But the love of benevolence makes our heart pass out of itself and exhale itself .... in all kinds of holy praises."

> **Application for Today**
>
> 1) Read Matthew 6: 19-24. How do the affections of one's heart either draw us closer to God or lead us farther from God?

Salesian Virtue: The Sign of True Prayer

People often think that our prayers end when we make the Sign of the Cross. In the Salesian Tradition our prayer should transform our hearts to desire to act in concrete and loving acts that help our neighbor experience the love of God we have just experienced in our prayer. Saint Francis de Sales does not want us to be people who only imagine ourselves doing good in prayer, but people who do what is good promptly, actively, and diligently.

In order to help us avoid forgetting to do the good we planned in prayer, Saint Francis urges us to make an examination of conscience each day to give ourselves the chance to fulfill any missed opportunity to do good. In our lives we may not always have the chance to do great deeds, but these prayerful exercises can help us "Do ordinary tasks extraordinarily well" and to "Live each day well!"

Saint Francis says the best way to accomplish this is to practice the "Little Virtues" of gentleness, humility, integrity and temperance. If we act with these virtues, then we will actually become more like Jesus, which is

Saint Francis de Sales directly helping the poor with gentleness and humility.

the goal of Christian prayer. This will let us know that we are actually listening to God rather than just talking to ourselves.[42]

Likewise, in the next page and throughout this book you will be asked to make real, measurable and concrete resolutions so some concrete good comes out of your prayer with God.

These resolutions should be specific as to time, manner and place such as: Tomorrow after dinner (*time*) I will thoroughly (*manner*) clean the kitchen (*place*) and do the dishes for my mom.

Application for Today

1) Read Matthew 7: 21-25. Why is it important for Christians to move beyond beliefs into loving actions?

The Christ • Immanuel • Word Made Flesh • Son of God • Alpha and Omega • LORD • Lamb of God
The Way, the Truth and the Life
JN 14:6

While coloring this icon of Jesus, use your imagination to see God's presence with you amidst your busy school day. Dwell upon good thoughts about God's love for you. Enjoy this moment free from normal school work.

Write a brief prayer in response to the state of your heart at the moment.

Write your resolution to practice virtue more promptly, diligently and often.

Considerations *(Write down one insight about God's goodness.)*

_____

_____

_____

_____

_____

_____

Affections *(Write a three sentence heartfelt, spontaneous prayer.)*

_____

_____

_____

Resolution *(Write a resolution that describes what you will do and when.)*

_____

_____

Word Art: *(Doodle a meaningful phrase from your prayer. See the example on page 110)*

The Direction of Intention

My God, give me the grace to perform this action with You and through love for You. In advance, I offer to You all the good that I may do and accept all the difficulty I may meet therein. Amen.

Word Art Example: "I am the way, the truth and the life." John 14:6
Fill in with color pencils or pens if you wish.

Notes

1. *Introduction to the Devout Life*, Part One, Chapter 3.
2. *40th anniversary of Dei Verbum*, Pope Benedict XVI. See Dei Verbum 25.
3. Celebrating the Year of Saint Paul June 28, 2008-June 29, 2009, Section Three.
4. *Introduction to the Devout Life*, Part Five, Chapter 18. Also see Saint Francis' Dedicatory Prayer at the start of the book.
5. *Introduction to the Devout Life*, Part Two, Chapter 17. This form of this quote is better suited for younger readers today than the exact quote from the Introduction to the Devout Life as translated by Father Joseph D. Bowler, OSFS and Father Lewis S. Fiorelli, OSFS.
6. *Letters of Spiritual Direction*, page 111.
7. *Introduction to the Devout Life*, Part One, Chapter 1.
8. *Introduction to the Devout Life*, Part One, Chapter 1.
9. *Letters of Spiritual Direction*, page 105.
10. *The Spiritual Directory*, Article 1.
11. *Introduction to the Devout Life*, Part Five, Chapter 18.
12. *Introduction to the Devout Life*, Part Three, Chapter 36.
13. *Introduction to the Devout Life*, Part Three, Chapter 36.
14. *Treatise on the Love of God*, Book Five, Chapter 9.
15. Selected Letters, 125 cited in *Selected Salesian Subjects*, page 28. This is one of those oft quoted Salesian sayings attributed to Saint Francis De Sales that eludes proper citation. The closest that I could come to finding this quote was from the passage I have cited here. "No do not be afraid; you are walking on the sea, surrounded by wind and water, but you are with Jesus: so what is there to fear?"
16. *Golden Counsels*, page 11.
17. *Introduction to the Devout Life*, Part Four, Chapter 13.
18. *Treatise on the Love of God*, Book Five, Ch. 9.
19. *Salesian Insight* cited in *Selected Salesian Subjects*, page 82. This comes from the papal decree naming Saint Francis de Sales a Doctor of the Church that makes my point about De Sales use of the *Song of Songs*. "It should not be overlooked that in these lucubrations especially in his interpretation of the *Canticle of Canticles*, many Scriptural puzzles involving moral and anagogical meanings are solved, difficulties explained, and obscure passages are bathed in new light."
20. *Introduction to the Devout Life*, Part Three, Chapter 41. This quote has been adapted slightly to make it gender inclusive and better suited for younger readers today. than the exact quote from the Introduction to the Devout Life as translated by Father Joseph D. Bowler, OSFS and Father Lewis S. Fiorelli, OSFS.
21. *Introduction to the Devout Life*, Part Three, Chapter 2.
22. *Introduction to the Devout Life*, Part Two, Chapter 14.
23. *Introduction to the Devout Life*, Part One, Chapter 1. Also see note 9 above.
24. *Introduction to the Devout Life*, Part Two, Chapter 19.
25. Selected Letters, page 44. Another of those oft quoted Salesian sayings attributed to Saint Francis de Sales that eludes the perfect match required for proper citation. Here I have provided the closest match I could find "In our self-scrutiny we should never aim at discovering whether we are imperfect, for this should never be a matter of any doubt. It follows that we should not be astonished to find ourselves imperfect, for we should never see ourselves other-wise in this life; nor should we let this upset us, as it cannot be helped, but rather let it be a cause for humility, for this is the way to correct our faults and gradually improve."
26. *Saint Francis de Sales: A Testimony* by Saint Chantal, page 63.
27. *Golden Counsels*, page 28.
28. *Introduction to the Devout Life*, Part Three, Chapter 1
29. *Little Virtues* cited in Selected Salesian Subjects, page 97. This is another one of those oft quoted Salesian sayings attributed to Saint Francis De Sales that eludes proper citation in the actual writings of Saint Francis de Sales.
30. *Praying with Francis de Sales*, page 13.
31. *Praying with Francis de Sales*, pages 14-15.
32. *Praying with Francis de Sales*, pages 16-17.
33. *Praying with Francis de Sales*, pages 17-18.
34. *Introduction to the Devout Life*, Part Two, Chapter 1.
35. *Introduction to the Devout Life*, Part One, Chapter 3.
36. *Praying with Francis de Sales*, page 19.
37. *Praying with Francis de Sales*, pages 19-20.
38. *Praying with Francis de Sales*, pages 21-22.
39. *Praying with Francis de Sales*, page 23.
40. *Praying with Francis de Sales*, page 24.
41. *Praying with Francis de Sales*, page 25-26.
42. *Praying with Francis de Sales*, page 26-27.

Bibliography

Dailey, Rev. Thomas F. *Praying with Francis de Sales.* Companions for the Journey series. Winona, MN: Saint Mary's Press, 1997.

Golden Counsels of Saint Francis de Sales. Tr. Peronne Marie Thibert, VHM. 1978.

Introduction to the Devout Life. Tr. Fr. Joseph D. Bowler, OSFS and Fr, Lewis Fiorelli, OSFS Rockford Illinois: TAN Books and Publishers, 1990.

Letters of Spiritual Direction. Tr. Peronne Marie Thibert, VHM: New York: Paulist Press, 1988.

Little Virtues. Hyattsville, MD: Oblate Helpers Guild, 1976

Marceau, William C., CSB, ed. *Salesian Insight.* n.d. (D-S)

Maxiums of Saint Francis De Sales. Hyattsville, MD: Oblate Helpers Guild, 1976.

New American Bible. Ed. Rev. Louis Hartmann, C.SS.R., Washington, DC: World Bible Publishers, Inc., 1987.

Pope *Benedict XVI. 40th anniversary of Dei Verbum. www.vatican.va/phome_en.htm., 1993.*

Saint Francis de Sales: A Testimony by St Chantal. Tr. Elizabeth Stopp. Hyattsville, MD: Institute of Salesian Studies, 1967.

Saltarelli, Bishop Michael. *Celebrating the Year of Saint Paul June 28, 2008-June 29, 2009. Catholic Diocese of Wilmington, January 2008.*

Select Salesian Subjects: Over 800 Passages by or about Francis de Sales and Jane de Chantal Selected from Fifty Sources. Compiled by Sr. Mary Grace Flynn, VHM. Stella Niagara, NY: De Sales Resources and Ministries, 2007.

Selected Letters. Tr. Elizabeth Stopp. New York: Harper and Brothers, 1960.

Spiritual Directory. Tr. Rev. John P. Connolly, OSFS. Wilmington, DE: Wilmington-Philadelphia Province of the Oblates of Saint Francis de Sales, 1974.

Treatise on the Love of God. 2 vol.. Tr. John K Ryan. Rockford, IL: TAN Books and Publishers, 1974.

Special Personal Acknowledgements

Meditation format adapted from Salesian Prayers of the Heart
by Father Michael Murray, OSFS, De Sales Spirituality Center

Salesian themed stained glass images from the Visitation Monastery in
Annecy, France, courtesy of Father Robert McGilvary, OSFS

Stained glass images "Live Jesus, Whom I Love" on page 104 and Saint Francis de Sales on page 105 from the
Oblate Chapel in Childs, MD, taken by Tom Vresics.

Stained glass image of the Sacred Heart of Jesus on page 106 from
Saints Simon and Jude Parish in West Chester, PA, taken by Tom Vresics

Iconic Lectio Description on page 46 by Neil Kane

Icon of Jesus on page 108 by Amy Vresics

Word Art example on page 110 by Tom Vresics

Proofread by Mary Ann Sianni

Publication Advisors: Betsy Diemer, Ed Gordon, Susan Gardner, Father Michael Donavan, OSFS.

Production Advisor Mary Facciolo

IT Advisors Brother Harry Schneider, OSFS., Chris Brower and Mike Mason.

Thanks to Bishop Michael Saltarelli, Bishop W. Francis Malooly and Bishop John Barres for their encouragement.

Thanks to Father William T. McCandless, OSFS for his support of this project.

God Be Praised!